Flourish

A Golden Age for Ceramics in Wales

Andrew Renton, Oliver Fairclough and Dr Rachel Conroy

Published by National Museum Wales Books, 2022

First published in 2022 by Amgueddfa Cymru,
Cathays Park, Cardiff, CF10 3NP, Wales.
© The National Museum of Wales
ISBN 978-0-72-000655-1

Design and typesetting: NB:Design
Printed by: Zenith Print

This publication has been assisted by a generous grant from Ceramica-Stiftung Basel.

This book was printed using certified materials (i.e. paper from sustainably managed forests), vegetable-based inks and water-based adhesives.

All rights reserved. No part of this publication may be reproduced, stored in a retrieval system or transmitted in any form or by any means, electrical, mechanical or otherwise, without the prior permission in writing of the National Museum of Wales, or the copyright owner(s), or as expressly permitted by law. Enquiries concerning reproduction outside the scope of the above should be sent to the Publishing Department, National Museum Cardiff, CARDIFF CF10 3NP.

The authors' moral rights have been asserted.

Foreword
By Lowri Davies

This book is a fresh, contemporary look at the ceramic and porcelain production that flourished in Wales between the 18th and 20th centuries.

As a maker, I've studied the work of the south Wales factories over many years, and there are many references to these collections in my work. I have created collections of my own based specifically on the work of the Nantgarw and Llanelli factories.

Nantgarw porcelain is unsurpassed. It is pure, transparent and exceedingly beautiful. The decoration of the objects is also remarkable, but it's the clay itself that stuns. As a maker who uses similar clay and has experienced losses in the kiln, reading about the extent of Billingsley's losses breaks my heart but his perseverance shows a character of true determination.

I was surprised to learn what an attraction craft tourism was, particularly in Swansea. We might think that decorating one's own pot for leisure is a contemporary activity, but it was on offer to tourists at Cambrian Pottery.

The Ewenny and Buckley potteries were founded on sites where clay already existed. By the time the factories described here were flourishing, clay was being imported from elsewhere. But their locations were still essential to their success. They needed to be able to use coal as energy, to transport goods to the potteries and the finished items to market. Today, there are many ceramics artists in south Wales, most notably around Cardiff and Pembrokeshire, attracted by education opportunities and the post-graduate community.

This book presents the historic ceramics collections in a new light, and I have certainly looked at familiar items with fresh eyes, as well as discovering new pieces for the first time. The jug decorated with a painting of a tiger, by Haynes, Dillwyn & Co., caught my attention – such a daring design (p. 29). Another piece that stands out for me is the pearlware honey pot, also by Haynes, Dillwyn & Co. (p. 36), so simple and yet so beautiful. I look forward to seeing it – and the jug – as I visit the collections, time and again, in the future.

Contents

1 | **Introduction**   1
Andrew Renton

2 | **The Early Years of the Swansea Pottery 1764-1789**   7
Andrew Renton

3 | **The Heyday of the Cambrian Pottery 1789-1824**   17
Andrew Renton

4 | **The Swansea China Works 1814-1826**   47
Oliver Fairclough

5 | **The Nantgarw China Works 1813-1814 and 1816-1823**   73
Oliver Fairclough

6 | **The Later Cambrian Pottery 1824-1870**   97
Rachel Conroy

7 | **The Glamorgan Pottery 1813-1838**   113
Rachel Conroy

8 | **The South Wales Pottery 1840-1922**   123
Rachel Conroy

9 | **The Leading Figures**   135

10 | **Manufacturers' Marks**   145

11 | **Further Reading**   153

The Swansea area in the 1790s, from George Yates's map of Glamorgan published by John Cary in 1799.

Flourish – A Golden Age for Ceramics in Wales

1 | Introduction

Amgueddfa Cymru's collection of Welsh factory ceramics is now the largest and most definitive such collection in the world. Starting life in 1882 at Cardiff's Free Library and Museum and transferred to the new National Museum after 1907, the collection has always aspired to be as complete a representation of the subject as possible, and continues to grow to this day.

This book is the first in several decades to embrace the full range of pottery and porcelain manufactured in south Wales between 1764, when the Swansea (later Cambrian) Pottery was established, and 1922, when Llanelli's South Wales Pottery (later known as the Llanelly Pottery) closed. Swansea is central to this story. Here, the Swansea Pottery was in operation by 1768 and finally closed in 1870, while on the same site the Swansea China Works produced porcelain between 1814 and 1826. Next door, from 1813 to 1838, was the Glamorgan Pottery. Beyond Swansea, the Nantgarw porcelain factory was active in two phases between 1813 and 1823. At Llanelli, the South Wales Pottery opened in 1840; when it closed in 1922 it was the last remaining significant Welsh pottery.

While the factories at Swansea, Nantgarw and Llanelli had distinctive local characteristics, the story of Welsh ceramics has a broader context. The rapid industrialization of south Wales in the eighteenth and nineteenth centuries played a substantial role in underpinning the development of Britain's empire. Had it not been for the area's close connections with the wider British and global economy, it is doubtful that the potteries and china works would have been established there.

The eighteenth century was a time of revolutionary transformation in the European ceramics industry. Change was led by the development of porcelain manufacture in Meissen in Germany in the early 1700s, and the creation in the Staffordshire pottery industry of the highly organized mass-production system pioneered by Josiah Wedgwood. These ground-breaking innovations had a profound impact throughout Europe. Factories everywhere emulated the success of the new types of porcelain and pottery.

On the continent the manufacture of true ('hard-paste') and artificial ('soft-paste') porcelain thrived thanks to committed royal and aristocratic patronage. However, in Britain the ceramics revolution needed to be commercially viable. This was possible, especially from the 1750s, thanks to a rapidly growing population and rising incomes. These stimulated demand from the 'middling classes' for durable, affordable, elegant ceramics which, through refined ornamental display and social rituals such as dining and tea drinking, helped them express the virtues of gentility and politeness.

South Wales was well placed to take advantage of this new economic climate for ceramics. It had plentiful supplies of high-quality coal, which was required in even greater quantity than clay. It also had easy access by sea to other essential raw materials – white clays from Devon, Dorset and Cornwall – and to the markets that were developing locally and in London, the rest of Britain and north America. When William Coles established his pothouse in Swansea in 1764, he saw that this thriving, internationally connected port, industrial centre and aspiring summer resort provided an excellent business opportunity.

Coles was not a potter, but a partner in a south-Wales tinworks. Like George Haynes and the Dillwyns after him, he was one of a new breed of commercially minded entrepreneurs who lacked expertise in ceramics but were attracted by Wedgwood's success to a business where money was to be made.

The exact role of such proprietors is not always clear; for Lewis Weston Dillwyn it varied from long periods of largely absentee management to intense personal involvement in ambitious projects. In 1806 his father William wrote that he had 'been much engaged in the application of his Chemical Knowledge' to the development of 'his lustre',[1] while in 1815 he started a notebook recording details of experimental porcelain bodies and glazes and wrote of 'a long fagging day's work at the Pottery.'[2]

By 1800, visitors to Swansea noted that its pottery was organized 'on Mr Wedgwood's plan.' This refers to the rational organization of Wedgwood's Etruria factory, opened in 1769 and quickly emulated by Staffordshire and the rest of Europe. Wedgwood's pioneering mass-production methods relied on economies of scale, division of labour, systemized production and wind-, water- or steam-powered mechanisation. All of this allowed him to increase output and keep prices down, while ensuring steady wages for a largely semi-skilled workforce.

It isn't clear exactly when 'Wedgwood's plan' was adopted in the Swansea Pottery, but in its early years, about 1770-1781, the Staffordshire master potter Ralph Ridgway was employed there, probably as works manager. Presumably, he brought knowledge of how to produce creamware, the newly fashionable 'Queen's Ware' that was then making Wedgwood's reputation and fortune.[3] In 1783, a sale notice for the Pottery said it had 'two excellent Water Mills ... for grinding the Flints', necessary for the advanced Staffordshire technique of adding ground flint to produce a stable white body. The same notice also advertised that 'The Country is very populous ... and Labour very cheap', suggesting that the Pottery was by then set up to work on Wedgwood's lines using semi-skilled workers.[4]

At this time, Staffordshire manufacturers were increasingly developing the newly invented bone china as a reliable, mass-market porcelain. By contrast, a few ambitious manufacturers emulated the high-art values of lavishly produced continental porcelain, in response to the demands of an elite metropolitan market. Like Derby, Worcester, Coalport and Spode, the Welsh porcelain factories competed with fashionable, expensive imports, from France in particular. This was especially true of Nantgarw, the idealistic project of William Billingsley that was the last gasp of the refined eighteenth-century soft-paste porcelain tradition, and never had a hope of being economically viable. At Swansea, Lewis Weston Dillwyn attempted to translate Billingsley's vision into something more practical, moving towards more reliable soaprock and bone porcelain recipes, but his porcelain venture was also a commercial failure.

From about 1790 factories everywhere came to rely, many of them almost exclusively, on underglaze transfer-printed decoration as their staple mass-market product. Spode led the way, building on the success of early blue-and-white chinoiserie designs, such as the ubiquitous 'Willow' pattern, with a vast array of new and often very sophisticated patterns. They ranged from flowers, birds and animals to historical and commemorative subjects and picturesque or fanciful views of India, Italy and elsewhere. The Swansea, Glamorgan and South Wales Potteries followed these wider market trends. Although ultimately none of these factories could survive overpowering competition from Staffordshire, particularly with the coming of the distribution system that railways offered, they did attempt to innovate. For example, when Lewis Weston Dillwyn took back control of the Cambrian Pottery in the 1820s, he introduced improvements to the pottery body and a new range of printed designs in a wider range of colours.

However, with few exceptions, little effort was made in south Wales to embrace the major developments of the Victorian period such as tile manufacture, colourfully glazed majolica, mid-century historicist styles or the later art pottery. In the late 1840s, Dillwyn's Etruscan Ware failed to halt the Cambrian Pottery's slow demise. Its closure in 1870 was no doubt hastened by competition from

---

[1] Jonathan Gray, *The Cambrian Company: Swansea Pottery in London 1806-1808* (2012), p. 144

[2] Oliver Fairclough, 'Lewis Weston Dillwyn and the Cambrian Pottery', Welsh Ceramics in Context Part 1 (2003), p. 220

[3] Jonathan Gray, 'The Ridgways in Swansea', English Ceramic Circle Transactions, 17 part 3 (2001), pp. 413-419

[4] Jonathan Gray, 'The Cambrian Pottery before 1802', Welsh Ceramics in Context Part 1 (2003), p. 24

local rivals such as the Ynysmeudwy Pottery (1845-1877), the Dyvatty Street Pottery (1840s-1892) and Calland and Company's Landore Pottery (about 1852-1856). The South Wales Pottery, despite its porcelain lithophanes in imitation of German examples, or its experiments with coloured bodies and spongeware, narrowly avoided extinction in 1875; a late blossoming of hand-painting in the popular Wemyss style couldn't fend off its final closure in 1922.

Throughout their histories, the Welsh pottery factories and china works relied significantly on the local markets. Swansea dishes and plates were used at the Pyle Inn before 1813 and at Carmarthen's Angel Inn in the 1840s. Swansea and Nantgarw porcelain was bought by numerous Welsh landowners and industrialists, from Lord Dynevor, one of the first recorded buyers of Swansea porcelain, to Sir Watkin Williams Wynn, who in about 1825 was disappointed as he could not obtain a complete Swansea service.

Tourists and visitors were also important customers. In the 1790s and 1800s Swansea promoted itself as an elegant seaside resort, and there are more tourist accounts of the Cambrian Pottery than of any other British ceramics factory of the period. Horatio Nelson visited in 1802 with Sir William and Emma Hamilton and ordered some pottery. Tourists could even decorate their purchases themselves, as members of the Alcock family from Ireland did in 1798. When porcelain was being produced, the former Swansea enameller Henry Morris recalled in 1850 that 'Many strangers came from a distance to purchase.'[5] Numerous picturesque local views appear on pottery and porcelain from Swansea and Nantgarw, perhaps painted to appeal to tourists or at their request.

But ceramics in south Wales were also made for export. Swansea Pottery, in its early decades, produced specially commissioned wares for Cornish customers, and probably competed with Bovey Tracey for markets in Devon, Dorset and Somerset. At times more concerted efforts were made to promote and distribute to key urban markets, particularly London and nearby Bristol. Essential to this strategy was the development of an image in keeping with the aspirations of the 'middling classes' and the taste of the wealthy elite.

The great pioneer of modern marketing methods for ceramics was, inevitably, Josiah Wedgwood, whose London showrooms from 1765 set an example of 'business, and amusement ... made to go hand in hand'. The example was followed in the late eighteenth century by several ambitious porcelain manufacturers and, between 1806 and 1808, by the Swansea (now 'Cambrian') Pottery, with its London warehouse, the Cambrian Company.[6] The name 'Cambrian' seems to have been a promotional gambit along the lines of Wedgwood's factory name 'Etruria' or the Liverpool pottery name 'Herculaneum'. When the Cambrian Company venture failed, Dillwyn sold his Swansea porcelain through well-established London specialists like Mortlock's of Oxford Street and Pellatt and Green of St Paul's Churchyard, who offered a similarly glamorous retail experience. Nantgarw porcelain reached its London customers in the same way.

Swansea ceramics also took advantage of the town's global trading links to reach an international market, just as potteries in north-east England, Liverpool, Yorkshire and Bristol exploited their maritime connections to north-west Europe and North America. Swansea had strong connections with ports in the Baltic, Italy and Iberia, to which it exported coal, and from 1830 with the Caribbean and South America, sources of the copper it smelted on a vast scale. However, the most important early connection appears to have been with the United States, and Philadelphia in particular, where George Haynes and William Dillwyn had strong business and family interests. When Haynes, a Philadelphia ship-owner, joined John Coles as partner in the Swansea Pottery in 1789, he considered that 'No situation that I know of is so eligible as this for the furnishing the United States with our wares.'[7]

A Cambrian Pottery plate painted by Mary Anne Alcock of Wilton Castle, County Wexford, 1798.
NMW A 31120

A Cambrian Pottery jug inscribed for Betsey Berriman Thomas of St Ives, 1804.
NMW A 30388

---

[5] Ernest Morton Nance, *The Pottery and Porcelain of Swansea and Nantgarw* (1942), p. 260

[6] Jonathan Gray, *The Cambrian Company: Swansea Pottery in London* (2012)

[7] Jonathan Gray, 'An American and an American Trader in Wales: Fresh Insights into the Cambrian Pottery, 1789-1810', *American Ceramic Circle Journal*, volume XVI (2007)

Like many British businesses of the eighteenth century, the Swansea Pottery benefited from money derived from the slave trade. George Haynes is recorded in Philadelphia as a slave-owner, and his business interests included significant involvement in the slave-based Caribbean sugar trade. In 1764 he married and settled on Sint Eustatius, the Dutch-owned island that was an important centre of the slave trade. He used this wealth to buy the Monckton Park estate near Wilmington, Delaware, and to invest in the Swansea Pottery. In contrast, William Dillwyn, who bought the Pottery in 1802 and whose son Lewis Weston went into partnership with Haynes, was a Quaker and prominent in the abolitionist movement in the American colonies and London from the early 1770s. He was a committee member of the Society for the Abolition of the Slave Trade, as was Josiah Wedgwood.[8]

Welsh ceramics, especially the porcelain produced at Nantgarw and Swansea between 1813 and 1826, have attracted the interest of collectors and connoisseurs since at least the early nineteenth century, and have been the object of academic study since at least the 1830s. Local pride has played a large part in encouraging this interest, and was reflected in the early use of Welsh-themed decorative subjects, whether bards and druids or celebrated local views. As early as 1813, south Wales auction notices singled out 'Swansea ware' for special mention, and Swansea newspaper *The Cambrian* was a ready mouthpiece for this civic pride. On 17 February 1817, *The Cambrian* featured an appeal for subscriptions to the 'Present to the Queen [Charlotte], From the Town and Neighbourhood of SWANSEA' of a specimen of Swansea porcelain, this 'being unrivalled for beauty and elegance.'

The qualities of Welsh ceramics, the porcelain in particular, were also quickly recognised further afield, and in the most discriminating circles. In London, the most important market, a key role was played by the city's leading china dealers, among which Mortlock's of Oxford Street was pre-eminent. From 1808 Mortlock's was Lewis Weston Dillwyn's first choice as agent for Swansea pottery and porcelain, and in that year Mrs Piozzi, born Hester Salusbury of Bachygraig, Flintshire, and better known as Dr Johnson's Mrs Thrale, urged a friend to go there to buy 'a beautiful specimen of South Wales china' (probably Cambrian Pottery pearlware). John Mortlock was behind advertisements for Swansea porcelain that appeared in London newspapers from July 1816, and in that same month he achieved the publicity coup of supplying a Swansea porcelain cabaret service ('a superb dejeune set') each to Princess Mary and Princess Charlotte. Mortlock later agreed with William Billingsley to take all the Nantgarw porcelain he could make available 'in the white' (undecorated), for decoration by London's finest porcelain painters. Magnificent Welsh dinner, dessert and tea services reached the highest echelons of society, with commissions from the likes of the second Marquess of Exeter, the banker Thomas Coutts and Adolphus Duke of Cambridge, brother to the Prince Regent.

In the late 1820s, the worth of the now defunct Welsh porcelain was already recognised by collectors. In 1829 an Abergavenny sale notice spoke of 'the celebrated Nantgarw china', while in 1832 Dionysius Lardner's *Cabinet Cyclopaedia* recorded of Nantgarw that 'Since the discontinuance of this establishment, the excellent quality of its wares has been justly estimated, and the prices which are now eagerly given by amateurs and collectors for pieces of Nungarrow porcelain, are out of all proportion greater than were originally demanded by the makers.'[9] This no doubt explains why in the 1830s and 1840s William Weston Young persisted in abortive attempts to revive the manufacture of Nantgarw porcelain, and why the second Marquess of Bute tried to persuade Thomas Pardoe's son William Henry to do likewise.

The Victorian pioneers of ceramic history, starting with Joseph Marryat in 1850, echoed Lardner's complimentary tone. These early accounts also benefitted from direct access to people who were involved in the industry in the early nineteenth century, or their descendants. Lewis Weston Dillwyn provided information not only to Marryat but also to his son's father-in-law, Sir Henry de la Beche, for the 1855 catalogue of the Museum of

A Nantgarw porcelain plate, about 1820, decorated in London and inscribed with the retailer's mark Mortlock. NMW A 38955

---

[8] Jonathan Gray, 'Bitter Sweet – Josiah Wedgwood and William Dillwyn's response to sugar and slavery in the eighteenth and nineteenth centuries', Proceedings of the Wedgwood International Seminar 2016, pp. 71-82

[9] Dionysius Lardner, Cabinet Cyclopaedia, Volume 26: A Treatise of the Progressive Improvement and Present State of the Manufacture of Porcelain and Glass (1832)

Practical Geology, whose collection (now at the Victoria and Albert Museum) contained examples of Welsh ceramics given by the Dillwyn family.[10] The first substantial book on the subject, William Turner's *The Ceramics of Swansea and Nantgarw* (1897), has in many respects been superseded by subsequent scholarship, but did preserve important oral history garnered while the industry's high point was still just within living memory.

The Museum of Practical Geology can perhaps claim to have been the first public collection to include examples of Welsh pottery and porcelain, but others soon followed. The collection of eighteenth-century ceramics given by Lady Charlotte Schreiber (better known in Wales as Lady Charlotte Guest, the translator of the *Mabinogion*) to the Victoria and Albert Museum in 1885 included several pieces of Swansea and Nantgarw porcelain. Sir Augustus Wollaston Franks's gifts to the British Museum in 1887 also included interesting examples of Welsh pottery and porcelain.

By this date, a public collection was already being formed in Cardiff. A display of Swansea and Nantgarw porcelain had featured at Cardiff's first Fine Art and Industrial Exhibition in 1870 and, following a second one in 1881, the exhibition's organizers presented twenty pieces of Welsh porcelain to the Cardiff Museum. From 1882 the Museum was committed to developing a representative collection of Welsh ceramics under the guidance of Robert Drane, a Cardiff chemist who was also a significant scientist and antiquarian and a distinguished collector of Worcester porcelain. Drane could make mistakes – for example in disagreeing with curator John Ward's view that Thomas Pardoe was a more significant decorator of Nantgarw porcelain than William Billingsley – but by 1912 he had created a collection that the National Museum's Annual Report described as 'probably the largest and most representative in existence … and certainly the best known and most consulted.'

As museum collections developed, private collecting also flourished. In 1897 Turner listed over sixty collections in south Wales and another dozen elsewhere. Wilfred de Winton's comprehensive collection of European porcelain included a significant representation of Welsh porcelain. However, the greatest of these collections in the first half of the twentieth century was that of Ernest Morton Nance, whose bequest of fifteen hundred pieces of Welsh pottery and porcelain in 1952 transformed the Museum's ceramics collection. A schoolteacher and solicitor who had retired to Cornwall, Nance published his monumental book *The Pottery and Porcelain of Swansea and Nantgarw* in 1942. He had long been frustrated by mistakes perpetuated by earlier scholars – including the National Museum, whose 1931 Welsh ceramics catalogue he annotated with remarks like 'wrong again' and 'same old error.' Although time has revealed that Nance made errors of his own, the meticulous and exhaustive documentary research that underpins his book is a valuable foundation.

As comprehensive as Nance's book and collection were, our understanding of Welsh ceramics has never stood still. Thanks to the more analytically object-focused publications of W. D. John, Rowland Williams and Sir Leslie Joseph, we now have a much more accurate appreciation of the porcelain made at Swansea and Nantgarw, even as newly discovered shapes and patterns continue to emerge. Fresh light has been shed on the history of the south Wales potteries, initially by W. J. Grant-Davidson, whose broadly reliable accounts of the early Swansea Pottery nevertheless propose some attributions that now appear speculative or even unwarranted, and by Helen Hallesy. The most significant recent contribution has been that of Jonathan Gray, who has combined careful analysis of objects with ground-breaking documentary research. He has not only established a more reliable chronology for the early products but also, and more importantly, illuminated the Swansea Pottery's active role in a broader economic picture, including its relationship with the Staffordshire potteries, its ambitious focus on the London market between 1806 and 1808, and – most interestingly of all – its close ties to North America. This new research and fresh thinking made this book both possible and desirable.

A pair of Cambrian Pottery bulb pots painted by William Weston Young, presented to the British Museum by Sir Augustus Wollaston Franks © The Trustees of the British Museum.

---

[10] Jonathan Gray, 'Presented by Mrs Dillwyn – Swansea pottery and porcelain and the Museum of Practical Geology', English Ceramic Circle Transactions, 28 (2017)

[11] Oliver Fairclough, 'Wilfred de Winton, Church and China in Edwardian Wales', Brycheiniog, XLVII, 2016, pp. 71-89

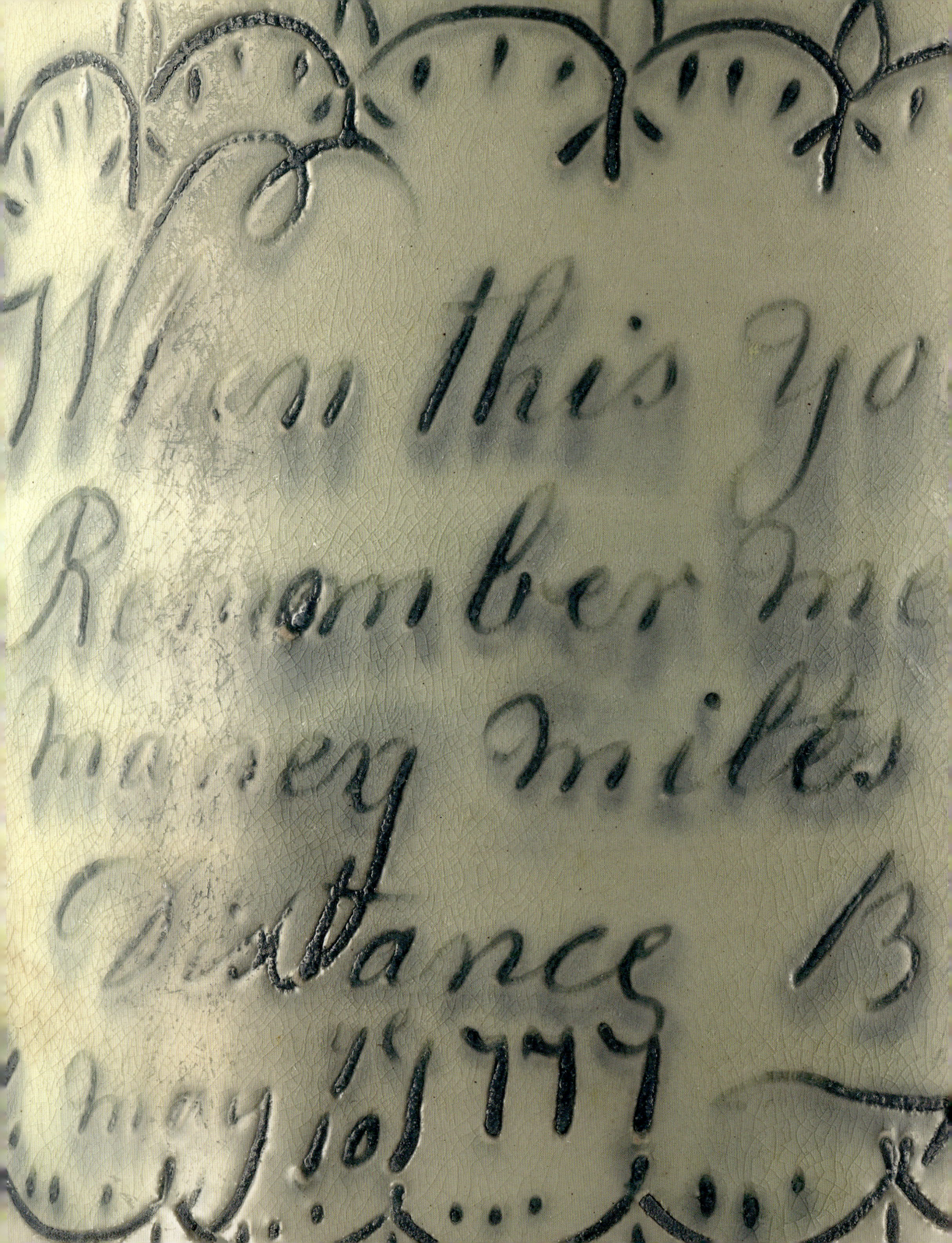

2 | The Early Years of the Swansea Pottery 1764-1789

In the 1760s the Burgesses of Swansea faced a dilemma. On the one hand, the town's maritime and industrial economy was flourishing; it was rapidly becoming the world's leading copper-smelting centre, soon to overtake Bristol as the most important port on the Severn estuary. On the other hand, the noxious atmosphere generated by copper smelting and other industries seriously undermined attempts to promote Swansea as a genteel seaside resort. The Burgesses were surely pleased, then, when on 19 September 1764 they granted a 41-year lease of the old Copper Works on the Strand to businessman William Coles, stipulating that he pull down the copper works and replace them with new buildings 'as necessary for the carrying on a Stone Ware or Earthen Ware manufactory' or 'any other work or manufactory except a copper or lead smelting house.'

Pottery had long been made in the area, at traditional potteries like Ewenny as well as Swansea itself. Coles, however, planned something new: a range of fine ceramics, of a type made fashionable and lucrative by the Staffordshire potteries. By late 1767 his new pothouse was ready to start manufacturing white, salt-glazed stoneware and cream-coloured earthenware, using local coal to fire white clays shipped from Cornwall, Devon and Dorset.

Our knowledge of the pottery produced at Swansea before Coles died in 1778 relies on fewer than a dozen documentary examples. These early pieces are so rare as to suggest that much unattributed British pottery of the period may in fact be unrecognised Swansea wares. William Dillwyn's diary for 15 July 1777 records his visit to Swansea's 'Pottery for Stone and Queen's ware a little above the town.' By this date, finely potted salt-glazed stoneware, hitherto the dominant product of the Staffordshire potteries, was already going out of fashion.

Swansea was one of the last places to make this Stoneware, and phased it out around 1778, perhaps on Coles's death. Creamware became the pottery's staple product, emulating Josiah Wedgwood's 'Queen's Ware' and possibly introduced by the Staffordshire master potter Ralph Ridgway, employed at the Pottery between about 1770 and 1781. High standards were achieved, and in 1775 Coles made plans to expand the Pottery.

Coles's sons, Rowland Pytt, Edward and John, ran the Pottery from 1778 to about 1789, probably without great enthusiasm to judge from their unsuccessful attempt in February 1783 to sell their 'very capital SET of WORKS, well calculated for the POTTERY, GLASS, or any other Business, wherein well constructed Cones are necessary.' This sale notice in The Morning Herald and Daily Advertiser noted that 'The present Proprietor accidentally became possessed of the Works.'

Between 1775 and 1783 the American War of Independence brought a general economic downturn, and very little identifiable Swansea pottery survives from this period. Nevertheless, some progress was made, and hand-painted decoration was introduced around 1781.

In 1788 John Flight of the Worcester porcelain factory wrote, 'I long to try a scheme of China Manufactory about Swansea', suggesting that the Coles brothers may then have tried again to sell the Pottery. Flight's idea came to nothing, but in 1789 the Pottery received fresh impetus and a new direction when John Coles went into partnership with the successful Philadelphia businessman George Haynes.

Tea canister, 1777

William Coles & Co, Swansea Potworks

Inscription probably by George Ridgway

Creamware

Height 10.7 cm

Inscribed Swansea potwork / May y^e 10 1777, incised

Purchased with assistance from Art Fund and Dr Graham Jenkins, 2015

NMW A 39563

Swansea potwork / May ye 10 1777 says the incised inscription, making this the second earliest object that we know for certain was made at the Swansea Potworks.[12] It is important evidence for what the earliest Swansea pottery looked like.

This may seem a humble, charmingly naïve object, but in south Wales in the 1770s it was something new and a desirable alternative to local country pottery. It is made of creamware, a refined pottery body made fashionable by Josiah Wedgwood and probably introduced to Swansea by the Staffordshire master potter Ralph Ridgway. The border pattern and inscription have been cut into the surface of the pot and coloured blue using cobalt oxide pigment. This 'scratch-blue' technique had been used in Staffordshire and elsewhere since about 1740, and was distinctly old-fashioned when Swansea used it in the 1770s.

The canister was most likely made as a gift, perhaps as a token of love or friendship. Tea was still an expensive and refined drink, commonly served by women hosting friends and guests. An object like this, delicately potted and accurately made, would have been an appropriate container for tea leaves on such an occasion. It was probably sealed with a cork or a cloth bung.

---

[12] The earliest is a salt-glazed stoneware flask dated 28th March 1768, in the collection of Swansea Museum

The Early Years of the Swansea Pottery 1764–1789

Jug, 1781

Attributed to John Coles & Co, Swansea Pottery

Creamware

Height 27.8 cm

Unmarked

Given in memory of Arthur Vaughan Williams, 1958

NMW A 30364

This is one of the most handsome pieces of early Swansea pottery, and among the first known examples with hand-painted decoration. It is finely painted in blue under the glaze with flowers and a series of elaborate border patterns. The inscription reads *Joseph Vaughan Melyngriffy / Success to Admrial Rodney / And His Majestys Navy / 1781*. With its elaborate moulded and interlaced double handle, the jug compares well with the high-quality creamware produced by Leeds and other ambitious new potteries of the period.

Melingriffith, beside the River Taff a few miles north of Cardiff, was the site of Harford, Getley and Company's iron and tinplate works, established in about 1750 and from 1770 managed by Joseph Vaughan (1736-1796). According to an unreliable family tradition, in 1781 Vaughan toured south Wales with his cousin John Vaughan of Dowlais (but more likely his younger brother John). It is said that while in Swansea they visited the Pottery and commissioned this large jug celebrating Admiral Rodney's controversial recent capture from the Dutch of the island of Sint Eustatius in the West Indies. They may have believed (wrongly) that General Sir John Vaughan, who played a significant role in Rodney's victory, was a kinsman.

Tea canister, about 1782
Attributed to John Coles & Co, Swansea Pottery

Creamware

Height 12.1 cm

Unmarked

Purchased, 1986

NMW A 30366

This tea canister demonstrates the technical advances and high standards at the Swansea Pottery by the early 1780s. Below the shoulder, complementing the hand-painted decoration in underglaze blue, are well-moulded scallop-shell edges and swags of flowers and leaves. Such refinement required sophisticated mould-making skills of the kind pioneered by the Staffordshire ceramics industry as it developed mass-production methods.

Another advanced Staffordshire technique in use at Swansea was the addition of ground flint to produce a high-quality, pale-coloured creamware body. An advertisement for the sale of the Pottery in *The Morning Herald and Daily Advertiser* in February 1783 mentions 'two excellent Water Mills ... for grinding the Flints.' This technology may have been introduced by experts from Staffordshire, such as master potter Ralph Ridgway, who was probably the Pottery's works manager during the 1770s.

Evidence for the date and purpose of this tea canister is provided by another similar one at Swansea Museum, which is inscribed *Green Tea / 1782*.

Tea canister, 1783

John Coles & Co, Swansea Pottery

Creamware

Height 13.8 cm

Unmarked

Given by Miss May Loveluck, 1961

NMW A 30365

The decoration of this tea canister reveals a range of influences. The scene painted on the back echoes the porcelain imported from China in huge quantities throughout the eighteenth century. However, it is more closely based on the loose imitations of Chinese porcelain landscapes that are found on English ceramics: on delftware, on porcelain and on the new type of white earthenware known as pearlware.

The border pattern round the shoulder is sophisticated, but its baroque or rococo style was old-fashioned in 1783. By contrast, the cartouche enclosing the date and the trailing husks to each side reflect the newly fashionable neo-classical style. The delicate beaded bands round the shoulder and foot add to the overall impression of an object intended to impress. Whoever Thomas Richards was, in 1783 the Swansea Pottery was able to supply him with a personalised object of considerable artistic ambition.

In the 1780s the English delftware industry was on its last legs, and many of its artists were looking for work elsewhere. The unidentified painter of this tea canister may have come to Swansea from a delftware pottery. The same artist decorated a number of objects dated between 1781 and 1783, including the jug made for Joseph Vaughan in 1781 (see p. 10).

Mug, 1786

Attributed to John Coles & Co, Swansea Pottery

Creamware

Height 12.6 cm

Unmarked

Acquired by exchange, 1920

NMW A 30367

The inscription reads *Mary Hopkins Her Cup 1786*. The heart-shaped motif suggests that it was presented to her as a betrothal or marriage gift.

It is not certain that the mug was made in Swansea but, given that it was discovered in Neath, this is the most likely possibility. Concrete evidence for the appearance of Swansea Pottery at this date is extremely scarce, but it is possible that the two half-pint mugs bought for threepence by the Rev. John Collins of Oxwich on 4 July 1782 looked a little like this.

The unusual 'powder blue' or 'soufflé' ground is not known on any other Swansea Pottery object of the eighteenth century. It appears to have been created either by dusting cobalt blue pigment onto the unglazed pot or by using the traditional technique of spraying the pigment through a tube. A paper template cut in the shape of a heart was applied to the surface as a mask, to create the white reserve that was painted with a stylised Chinese landscape. The finished result resembles imported Chinese porcelain and imitations of it made at British factories like Bow or Worcester in the 1750s and 1760s.

Teapot, 1788

John Coles & Co, Swansea Pottery

Creamware

Height 12.1 cm

Unmarked

Found in collection, 1955

NMW A 30368

This is one of a number of objects made at the Swansea Pottery between 1787 and 1789, all painted in the same distinctive style with inscriptions, dates and decorative motifs. This teapot is one of several of these objects which also feature a well-painted landscape in a Chinese style.

We don't know who the painter of these objects was, but it wasn't the artist who painted Joseph Vaughan's jug in 1781 (p. 10) or Thomas Richards's tea canister in 1783 (p. 12). This artist probably trained in one of Britain's delftware or porcelain factories, and can be recognised by his (or possibly her) idiosyncratic habit of putting a semi-colon between personal names. The teapot is also decorated with stylised flowers and insects, and scrolling and scalloped borders, which are typical features of this artist's style.

Nothing has yet been discovered about Clement Morris, the owner named in the teapot's painted inscription. He is perhaps more likely to have lived at Merthyr Mawr near Bridgend than in the rapidly growing industrial town of Merthyr Tydfil.

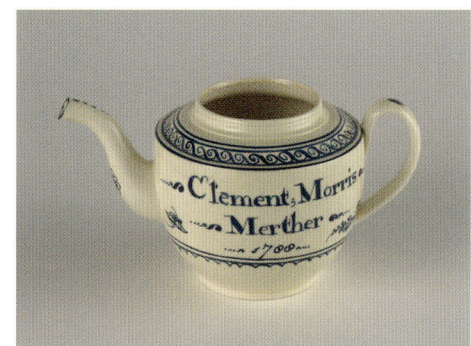

Dish, 1788

John Coles & Co, Swansea Pottery

Creamware

Diameter 32.2 cm

Unmarked

Bequeathed by Ernest Morton Nance, 1952

NMW A 30369

This dish belongs to the same distinctive group as Clement Morris's teapot (p. 14), all painted at the Swansea Pottery between 1787 and 1789. The moulded, lobed shape imitates a form that was first fashionable in silver in the 1730s, but which by the 1750s had become a standard shape for silver and ceramic plates and dishes and remained popular into the nineteenth century. Given the size of this dish and the inscribed name, it was probably used more for show than for practical purposes.

The border pattern of dark blue scrolls on a lighter blue wash is a characteristic of this group of Swansea objects. However, a design similar to the border round the centre has also been found on shards excavated at the site of the Bovey Tracey pottery in Devon, suggesting that design influences passed one way or the other between the two potteries. Indeed, the trade across the Bristol Channel was clearly important to the Swansea Pottery, bringing the fine white clays the Pottery needed and, in the other direction, opening up a market for its finished products. Some objects painted in the style of this dish have inscriptions referring to places in Cornwall and north Devon.

3 | The Heyday of the Cambrian Pottery 1789-1824

In early 1789, ship-owner and businessman George Haynes was retiring from his business interests in Philadelphia, then America's largest and most important city. He had bought into the Swansea Pottery, and was running it in partnership with John Coles. Inspired by the success of Josiah Wedgwood, Haynes set about expanding and remodelling the Pottery. As visitors and local guidebooks in the 1790s and early 1800s attested, he reorganized the Pottery 'on Mr Wedgwood's plan', creating a complex arrangement of discrete spaces for each specialised process, from the 'Engine lathe room' and the 'Black Room' for making black basalt, to rooms for throwing, making plates and dishes, printing, modelling and painting (see right).

Haynes rebranded it the Cambrian Pottery and invested £1,500 in improving its wares, emulating the latest fashions from Staffordshire. These included the new pearlware body, a whiter type of pottery with a bluish glaze perfected by Wedgwood in 1779, and dry-bodied (unglazed) stoneware such as black basalt, perfected by Wedgwood in about 1768. Transfer-printed decoration was introduced, and the standard of hand-painting improved with the help of experts such as engraver Thomas Rothwell, chief painter Thomas Pardoe and modeller George Bentley.

This was a shrewd time to invest. Britain's trade with the United States was improving, and Haynes envisaged a potentially lucrative export business to Philadelphia. Just like potteries in north-east England, Liverpool, Yorkshire and Bristol, Swansea could exploit its maritime connections to reach an international market in north-west Europe and North America. In March 1790 Haynes wrote to an American correspondent 'No situation that I know of is so eligible as this for furnishing the United States with our wares.'

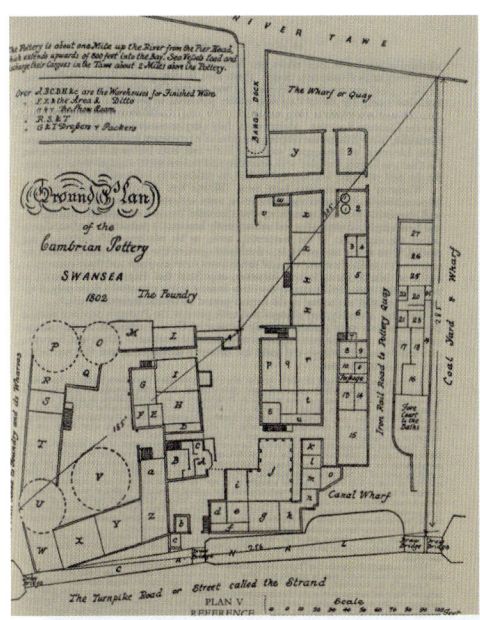

Plan of the Cambrian Pottery in 1802, reproduced from Ernest Morton Nance, *The Pottery and Porcelain of Swansea and Nantgarw* (1942).

In 1802 William Dillwyn, a Pennsylvania Quaker with family links to Haynes, bought the Pottery's leases. His son, Lewis Weston, took over in partnership with Haynes, and the Dillwyns invested £7,000 in new improvements. The younger Dillwyn was a naturalist and antiquarian of some note, with political and charitable interests as well, so generally managed the Pottery at arm's length. From time to time, however, if business required – or more particularly if his scientific interest was stimulated – his devotion to the Pottery was intense.

In the first two decades of the nineteenth century the Cambrian Pottery reached its apogee, and Dillwyn had a particular personal interest in the two ventures that stand out as the peaks of its achievement: the Cambrian Company warehouse, which operated at 64 Fleet Street, London from 1806 to 1808, and the decade of porcelain manufacture from 1814. Pottery produced for the London warehouse shows how Dillwyn's vision and leadership transformed the range and quality of the Cambrian Pottery's wares. Handsome new ornamental and functional shapes, and the distinctive, high-quality hand-painting of Thomas Pardoe and William Weston Young, established Swansea as one of Britain's most ambitious and accomplished potteries.

However, it seems the Cambrian Company was not a financial success, and with its closure the Pottery's fortunes were on the ebb. In 1809, with the national economy ailing and demand for high-quality painted earthenware apparently waning, Thomas Pardoe left to set up his own business in Bristol. Matters were made worse by the breakdown in Dillwyn's relationship with Haynes, who left in 1810 and, in 1813, right next door to the Cambrian Pottery, established the rival Glamorgan Pottery (see Chapter 7). Dillwyn complained that 'the Profits fell very short of the great expectations which G.H. [Haynes] had held out.'

Dillwyn entered a new partnership in 1810, with Timothy and John Bevington, trading as Dillwyn & Co. until 1817. They maintained high standards, with the emphasis on transfer-printed decoration. By 1817 Dillwyn was running an increasingly profitable business, making around £2,000 a year.

Punch bowl, about 1790-1800
Possibly Cambrian Pottery (Coles & Haynes)
Pearlware
Diameter 28.2 cm, height 12.7 cm
Unmarked
Given by W. J. Grant-Davidson, 1994
NMW A 32261

It is this bowl's decoration that suggests it was made in Swansea. Inside, we see a large swan swimming between two rocks, with a pike rising below. The 'swan on the sea' might be a rebus, referring to the place of manufacture. The pike is possibly a reference to the Pike family of Corfe Castle in Dorset, who operated as clay merchants from 1760, and in the early nineteenth century traded between Poole and Swansea using a ship called *Swan*. They also supplied Staffordshire potteries, including Minton.

Outside, there is a hand-painted Chinese-style landscape, a popular feature of late eighteenth-century British pottery.

This bowl illustrates the difficulty of identifying early products of the Cambrian Pottery. Most of them must have been unmarked, and probably survive in larger numbers than is generally recognised, misidentified as 'English' pottery.

The Heyday of the Cambrian Pottery 1789-1824

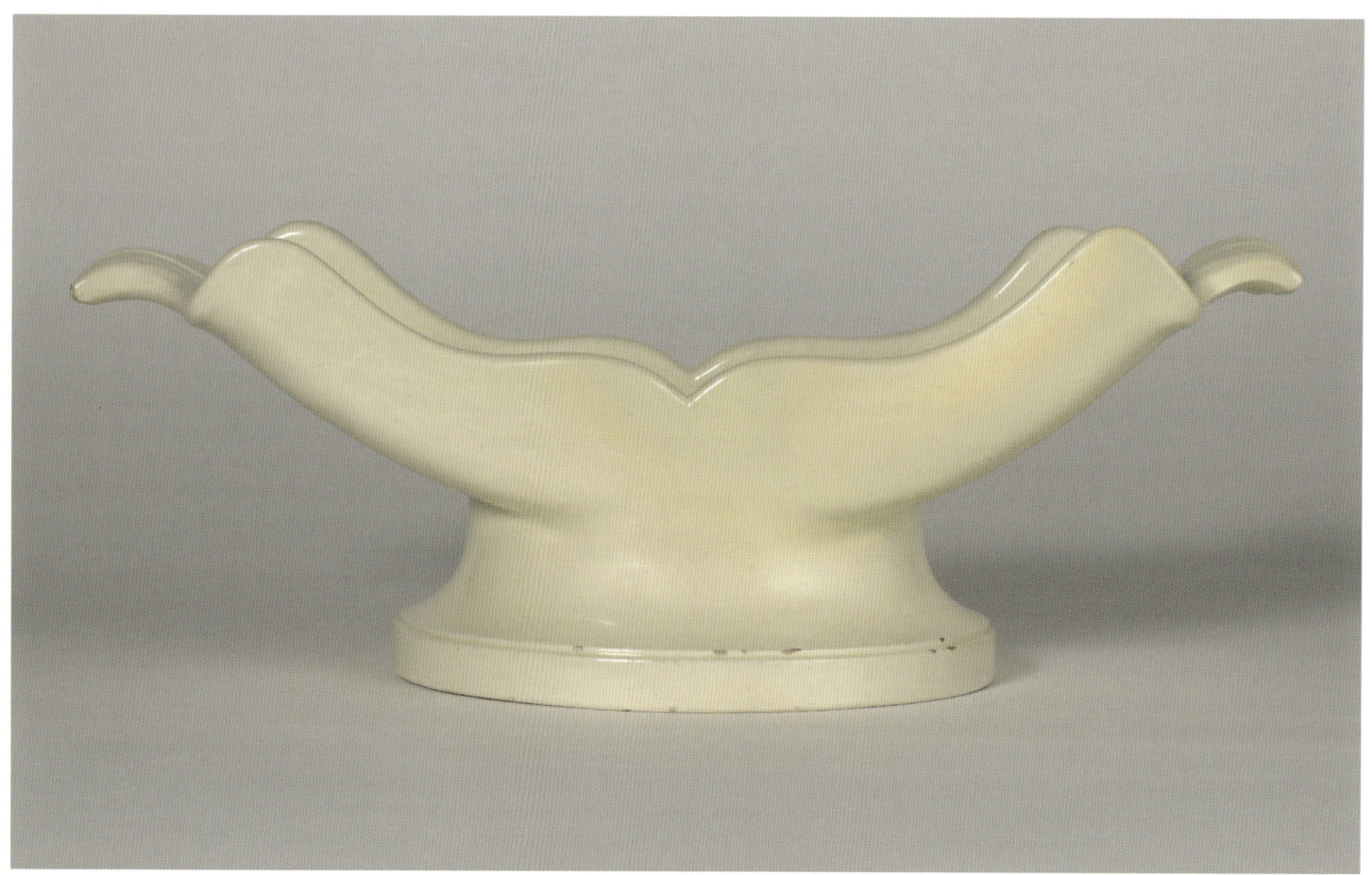

Cheese cradle, about 1802-1811
Haynes, Dillwyn & Co.
Creamware
Length 35 cm
Mark: SWANSEA, impressed
Purchased, 1951
NMW A 30371

Dairy, kitchen and dining wares of cream-coloured earthenware were a staple product of the Swansea Pottery in the late eighteenth and early nineteenth centuries. These were utilitarian objects for everyday use, so rarely survive today. This cheese cradle is designed to hold a circular cheese on its side so that wedge-shaped pieces can be cut from it. The curved handles allow it to be carried while holding a cheese.

These functional wares were probably made mainly for the local market. The landowner Thomas Johnes of Hafod near Aberystwyth, for example, was keen to improve his dairy and bought creamware milk pans made in Swansea, possibly as early as the late 1780s. In 1800, he published *A Cardiganshire Landlord's Advice to his Tenants,* in which he wrote, 'What pans I use are made at the pottery in Swansea; they are of the yellow ware; and though their glazing is made of lead yet the operation they undergo in the furnace makes them less dangerous.'

Plate, 1794

Coles & Haynes

Pearlware, transfer-printed with painted inscription

Diameter 21 cm, height 1.4 cm

Unmarked

Purchased, 1962

NMW A 30391

Transfer-printed decoration may have been introduced at the Swansea Pottery in the late 1780s, but this plate is the earliest known example that can be securely dated. This innovation has generally been associated with the arrival in Swansea of the copper-plate engraver and enameller Thomas Rothwell (1740-1807), who had previously worked in his native Liverpool and the Staffordshire potteries.

Rothwell engraved copper plates for the Cambrian Pottery until about 1791, but we don't know which specific patterns he was responsible for. He had left Swansea by 1794, so this 'elephant and howdah' pattern may be the work of another engraver. Rothwell also engraved local views, some of them printed onto plaster and given Swansea pottery frames.

From the early 1790s, transfer-printed decoration became a staple Swansea product. This didn't mean a move towards cheaper, mass-market decoration, as the process was actually more expensive than hand-painting. John Henry Manners, 5th Duke of Rutland, visited the Pottery in August 1797 and described the process of printing from copper plates onto paper which was wrapped round the wares to transfer the image. He noted: 'Those that are printed are infinitely superior to those that are only painted.'

The Heyday of the Cambrian Pottery 1789-1824

Jug, 1801

Coles & Haynes or Haynes & Co.

Pearlware, transfer-printed with painted inscription

Height 15.2 cm, diameter 13.3 cm

Unmarked

Bequeathed by Ernest Morton Nance, 1952

NMW A 30387

Printed under the glaze in brown, the decoration features Chinese garden scenes with figures holding parasols and a boy fishing with a net. These are based on the highly influential engravings of Jean Pillement, which were used in Robert Sayer's *The Ladies Amusement*, first published in 1760, and made such whimsical chinoiserie designs extremely popular in the late eighteenth century.

When John Henry Manners, 5th Duke of Rutland, visited the Cambrian Pottery in 1797 he was struck by 'a sort of Brown colour, lately discovered by some person in London, which is much used here.' Other than the more usual blue, Swansea also used black for its underglaze transfer-printed decoration.

The jug is inscribed for Samuel and Grace Calley, possibly Samuel Calley and Grace Wakeham of Devon, who married in Dartmouth on 3 December 1795. If so, this is one of a series of documentary jugs from as early as 1797 that show how many of the Cambrian Pottery's products at this period were exported across the Bristol Channel.

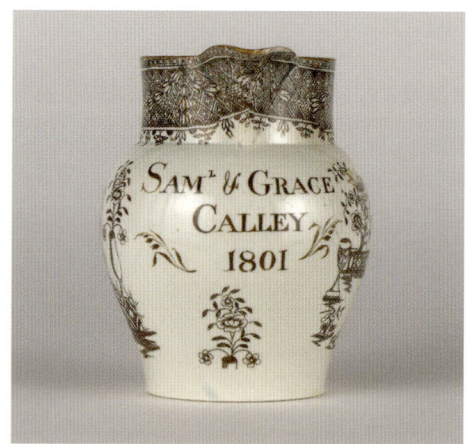

Figures of Mark Antony and Cleopatra

Haynes, Dillwyn & Co., about 1810-1815 (Mark Antony) and about 1805 (Cleopatra)

Yellow-glazed earthenware; black basalt

Mark Antony: height 19.3 cm, length 32.4 cm
Cleopatra: height 21.6 cm, length 28.9 cm

Marks: Mark Antony unmarked; Cleopatra SWANSEA, impressed

Bequeathed by Ernest Morton Nance, 1952
Bequeathed by Kildare S. Meager, 1965

NMW A 30798 & 30394

The Cambrian Pottery made paired figures of Mark Antony and Cleopatra in yellow-glazed earthenware and black basalt. One basalt figure of Cleopatra is incised 'G. Bentley, Swansea 22nd May, 1791', so the high-quality modelling was by George Bentley, the Pottery's chief modeller. Bentley remained in Swansea until his death in 1810, and so probably modelled many of the more complex forms, such as the vases and ornamental wares designed in about 1805-1807 for the Cambrian Warehouse in London.

Basalt is a black unglazed stoneware that was perfected by Wedgwood in 1768 and introduced at Swansea from about 1790, when an 'Egypt Black Sugar Box' appeared in a receipt for purchases by Reverend John Collins of Oxwich. Very few marked Swansea examples survive, but it must have been made in significant quantity.

The figure of Cleopatra is based on a well-known Roman marble sculpture of the sleeping Ariadne in the Capitoline Museum in Rome, which at the time was thought to represent Cleopatra.

Jug, 1800

Coles & Haynes

Painted by Thomas Pardoe

Pearlware

Height 24.9 cm, diameter 18.5 cm, width 25.1 cm

Inscribed *Mr. Husbands / Swansea / 1800*

Bequeathed by Ernest Morton Nance, 1952

NMW A 30373

The texts, inscribed by Thomas Pardoe, the Cambrian Pottery's chief painter, read *TRADE & AGRICULTURE; SUCCESS TO NY* and *PRESERVING OUR COUNTRY RELIGION, (AND LAWS,) UNITED AND FIRM WE SUPPORT THE GOOD CAUSE.* The 'good cause' was the war with France, and these patriotic sentiments would have pleased Pardoe. Like his father-in-law Roger Landeg, Pardoe was an enthusiastic volunteer in the Swansea, Gower and Kilvey Infantry Legion. He painted its colours in 1801 and carried out 'special and important duties' that may have included coastal scouting.

The themes of trade and agriculture were dear to Jaques Husbands, whose monogram, *JMH*, appears under the spout. Husbands was a 'stuffmaker' (a worsted manufacturer) and landowner, originally from Coventry. He lived near Roger Landeg, and may have known Pardoe personally. He also owned a 'convenient and genteel' house and garden in Frog Street in Swansea.

A Cambrian Pottery pearlware jug, inscribed *SWANSEA / VOLUNTEERS* by Thomas Pardoe, about 1800-1802.

Mug, about 1805-1806

Haynes, Dillwyn & Co.

Painted, probably by Thomas Pardoe

Pearlware

Height 15.9 cm, diameter 11.2 cm

Unmarked

Given by the Friends of Amgueddfa Cymru, 1956

NMW A 30395

His naval victories against France made Admiral Horatio Lord Nelson (1758-1805) a national hero, and his death at Trafalgar in 1805 was a major event. The Cambrian Pottery made a number of objects commemorating him, including jugs and mugs like this one bearing his portrait. The stock of the Cambrian Warehouse in London in 1808 contained a number of 'very handsome' jugs depicting Nelson.

The gilding by Thomas Pardoe includes not only the portrait's border but also on one side acorns, flowers, foliage and a butterfly, and on the other a wheat ear and an insect. The portrait is in the meticulous style of William Weston Young but could well be Pardoe's work. The image derives from Lemuel Francis Abbott's portrait of 1797, engraved in mezzotint in 1798, but the coarser face on the mug is more of a true likeness. This may reflect Pardoe's personal memory, given that as a military volunteer Pardoe may well have met Nelson when he visited the Cambrian Pottery in 1802 on his way to review the dockyard at Milford Haven.

The Heyday of the Cambrian Pottery 1789-1824

Jug and plate

Haynes, Dillwyn & Co., 1804 and about 1802-1811

Pearlware

Jug: height 17.5 cm, diameter 11.6 cm
Plate: diameter 24.8 cm, height 1.9 cm

Marks: Jug unmarked; plate *SWANSEA*, impressed

Bequeathed by Ernest Morton Nance, 1952

NMW A 30705 & 30707

The jug's printed design shows an armed brig in full sail over an arrangement of naval motifs including a mermaid's head, cannon, anchor, trident, drum and various weapons. Brigs were swift two-masted vessels suitable for naval or mercantile use. The plate features an armed one-masted cutter, a type of workboat designed for speed and typically used to ferry harbour pilots to and from large vessels. The prints reflect the importance of shipping to Britain's economic and military might at the time. Ship prints like this were popular on British pottery in the late eighteenth and early nineteenth centuries, and were produced by potteries in Staffordshire, Liverpool and north-east England, often for export to the United States. It was natural that a pottery in a major port like Swansea would create its own range of ship prints.

The inscription on the jug reads *When this you See Remember me / And bear me in your mind / Tho' many leagues we distant be / Speak of me as you find / Wm. SAUNDERS / 1804*. It seems likely that this jug was commissioned by a William Saunders as he was about to go to sea.

The designs are transfer-printed under the glaze in blue and purple, using pigments derived from oxides of cobalt and manganese.

Vase for dried flowers, about 1805
Haynes, Dillwyn & Co.
Black basalt
Height 31.6 cm, diameter 14.3 cm
Mark. *SWANSEA*, impressed
Bequeathed by Ernest Morton Nance, 1952
NMW A 30783

The vase is decorated with four sprigs of grouped female figures, moulded separately in low relief and applied to the surface. One of these is Britannia with a lion, pointing to Fame playing a trumpet. The others feature a woman crowning a bust with a laurel wreath, another weeping over an urn on a column and a third holding a lighted candle. These, and the black colour, suggest that this is a mourning piece, possibly commemorating the death of Nelson in 1805 or of General Ralph Abercrombie at the battle of Alexandria in Egypt in 1801.

This is a sophisticated object, inspired by the example of Josiah Wedgwood's products, and it illustrates the high standards achieved by the Cambrian Pottery. It was precisely turned on a lathe to ensure an elegant classical vase form, with fluting produced by a specialist engine-turning lathe of the type pioneered by Wedgwood in about 1763.

Vase and cover, about 1805
Haynes, Dillwyn & Co.
Painted by Thomas Pardoe
Pearlware
Height 30.2 cm, diameter 19 cm
Mark: *CAMBRIAN*, painted in gold
Bequeathed by Ernest Morton Nance, 1952
NMW A 30554

This is an outstanding example of Thomas Pardoe's skills. The vibrant spray of a rose, iris and other flowers, complete with a butterfly, reflects his training at the Derby porcelain factory in the 1780s. This is also seen in the complex *caillouté* ('pebbled') gilding that covers the vase's deep blue ground. This pattern, pioneered on Sèvres porcelain in the 1760s and still fashionable half a century later, was a speciality of Pardoe's.

The *CAMBRIAN* mark in Pardoe's script may indicate that the vase was destined for sale at the Cambrian Warehouse in London, Dillwyn's ambitious attempt to break into the London market. This venture stimulated a repertoire of sophisticated new products, coherent in quality and style.

Jug, about 1805
Haynes, Dillwyn & Co.
Painted by Thomas Pardoe
Pearlware
Height 24.5 cm, diameter 19.6 cm
Mark: SWANSEA, painted in gold
Given by F. Emile Andrews, 1922
NMW A 30556

As chief painter at the Cambrian Pottery, Thomas Pardoe had a remarkably wide repertoire, ranging from the botanical decoration for which he is perhaps best known to zoological subjects, from landscapes and figures to chinoiserie and classical themes, armorials and gilding patterns.

Pardoe brought a lively individuality to the best of the Pottery's products, drawing on printed sources but using his own imagination to generate more complex compositions. This tiger is an accurate copy of an engraving by James Heath in George Shaw's *General Zoology* of 1800,[13] where it is described as 'the most beautiful, but most destructive of quadrupeds.' By contrast, the landscape with rocks, palms and other trees appears to be Pardoe's own invention.

This jug is one of three recorded Swansea tiger jugs, which may originally have formed an impressive set in graduated sizes. The larger one (height 26.8 cm) is painted by a different artist, probably William Weston Young, and has a *CAMBRIAN* mark painted in gold. The third jug has a painted *SWANSEA* mark, but its whereabouts and size are unknown.

---

[13] George Shaw, *General Zoology* (1800), Volume 1 Part 2

The Heyday of the Cambrian Pottery 1789-1824

Two mugs, 1803-1806

Haynes, Dillwyn & Co.

Painted by William Weston Young

Pearlware

Bard: height 15.5 cm, diameter 11.3 cm

Druid: height 15.5 cm, diameter 11.5 cm

Mark: *SWANSEA*, impressed

Given by Wyndham D. Clark, 1951

Given by W. J. Grant-Davidson, 1994

NMW A 30118 & 32245

In the late eighteenth and early nineteenth centuries British intellectuals developed a fascination with ancient Welsh culture, in particular its language, literature and music. For this reason, they saw bards and druids as central figures in Wales's Celtic heritage. Attempts to cultivate a separate identity for Wales included a revival of the Eisteddfod tradition, the founding of groups like The Honourable Society of Cymmrodorion and, in London in 1792, the establishment of the Gorsedd of the Bards by the radical romantic poet Iolo Morganwg (Edward Williams, 1747-1826).

The ideal of the Welsh bard as a champion of British liberty was given artistic expression by Thomas Gray in his widely influential poem *The Bard* (1755). This described the last Welsh bard cursing the invading army of Edward I of England, and inspired such iconic images as Thomas Jones's painting *The Bard* of 1774 and another by Philippe J. de Loutherbourg in 1784. An engraving of the latter seems to be the ultimate source for the Swansea bard mugs, of which several examples survive, painted either in sepia monochrome or in full colours. However, this druid mug, inscribed *Druid* in Young's script, is the only known example.

Gray's Bard after Philippe J. de Loutherbourg, frontispiece to Edward Jones, *Musical and Poetical Relicks of the Welsh Bards* (1784).

Two jugs, about 1805

Haynes, Dillwyn & Co.

Painted by Thomas Pardoe

Pearlware

Left: height 19.1 cm, diameter 15.3 cm
Right: height 18.8cm, diameter 14.3 cm

Unmarked

Bequeathed by Ernest Morton Nance, 1952. Purchased with funds given by Dr Graham Jenkins in memory of Mrs Hilda Rose Jenkins late of Ynysybwl, 2013

NMW A 30399 & 39527

These views, of Mumbles lighthouse and the hall at Caerphilly Castle, are identified by inscriptions in gold by Pardoe: *View near Swansea* and *Hall Caerphilly Castle*. Swansea Bay and Caerphilly Castle were popular tourist destinations in the 1790s and 1800s, as was the Cambrian Pottery itself, so it is possible that these two jugs were made as souvenirs for well-to-do travellers on a picturesque tour of south Wales.

No print sources have been identified for these views, so it is likely that they are based on Pardoe's own observation. The view of Mumbles lighthouse through a natural arch in the cliffs near Oystermouth was described in 1804 as 'admirably picturesque' and the lighthouse itself as 'only accessible on foot at low water, and even then the ascent is not perfectly easy.'[14] The imposing ruins of Caerphilly Castle feature in a number of topographical prints of this period.

---

[14] E. Donovan, *Descriptive excursions through south Wales and Monmouthshire, in the year 1804, and the four preceding summers* (1805), volume 2

The Heyday of the Cambrian Pottery 1789-1824

Cream tureen and stand, about 1805

Haynes, Dillwyn & Co.

Painted by Thomas Pardoe

Pearlware

Tureen and cover: height 17.9 cm

Unmarked

Bequeathed by Ernest Morton Nance, 1952

NMW A 30518

This cream tureen from a dessert service is typical of the fine botanical decoration for which Thomas Pardoe is best known. He made meticulous pencil and watercolour copies of his print sources to use as references. His scientific sources were William Curtis's *Botanical Magazine* and Henry Andrews's *Botanist's Repository*.

The flowers on this tureen are all identified by inscriptions and based on engravings published by Curtis in 1790, 1791, 1797 and 1798. They are 'Mediterranean Stock', 'Many Flowered Zinnia', 'Scarlet Flowered Cyrilla', 'Martinico Iris' and 'Peerless Daffodil'.

In producing botanical services of this kind, the Cambrian Pottery was following a fashion pioneered by the Royal Copenhagen porcelain factory in 1790 and followed by English porcelain factories like Derby in the same decade.

Comport, or centre dish; comport, bowl and cream tureen, about 1805

Haynes, Dillwyn & Co.

Painted by William Weston Young
Painted by Thomas Pardoe

Pearlware

Top: height 12.8 cm, length 32.1 cm
Right: Comport: height 13.3 cm, length 25.7 cm
Bowl: diameter 19.7 cm, height 4.1 cm
Tureen: height 14 cm, length 22.3 cm

Mark: *SWANSEA*, impressed

Given by Kildare S. Meager, 1947. Purchased, 1988

NMW A 30532, 30492, 30488, 30491

These pieces from two different dessert services illustrate the contrasting styles of William Weston Young and Thomas Pardoe. Top is a comport, or centre dish, from a service inscribed with the unidentified monogram *RIR*. The golden eagle, copied from an engraving published in 1795 in William Lewin's *The Birds of Great Britain*, is painted by Young in his characteristically painstaking style, the outlines crisply drawn and colours and textures depicted with great precision.

The others are pieces from a service originally owned by Thomas Edmondes of the Old Hall, Cowbridge. Pardoe copied all the birds from either Thomas Bewick's *British Birds* (1797-1804) or Lewin's *The Birds of Great Britain*, although they are painted in a broader style with less concern for scientific accuracy. The comport features goldfinches, the bowl a lesser spotted woodpecker and the tureen a treecreeper, redstart, whinchat and willow wren.

Pardoe copied prints in pencil and watercolour before 'pricking' them for transfer to pottery. This process removes the skill of painting outlines, so what we conventionally take to be Pardoe's painting might sometimes be the work of less skilled hands copying his models.

The Heyday of the Cambrian Pottery 1789-1824

Garniture of two vases and a match pot, about 1805

Haynes, Dillwyn & Co.

Painted by Thomas Pardoe

Pearlware

Vases: height 21 cm, diameter 11 cm
Match pot: height 18.4 cm, diameter 8.8 cm

Mark: SWANSea, painted in gold on one vase

Purchased, 1992 (Sir Leslie Joseph Collection)

NMW A 31122-31124

These are unique examples of this style of decoration by Pardoe. The cartouches on one side contain chinoiserie scenes with figures and buildings, those on the other side contain flowers painted in red. The decoration, and the shapes, echo Chinese porcelain originals. The scale-patterned ground in underglaze blue and the enamelled figure scenes are reminiscent of later eighteenth-century Chinese export porcelain decorated in the so-called 'Mandarin' palette.

The two baluster vases have probably lost their covers, and the full set may originally have comprised three such vases along with two match pots. This would match the description of one of the lots in the Christie's sale of the Cambrian Warehouse stock on 22 April 1808: 'Three vases and covers painted with figures and 2 match pots.'[15]

The contrasting styles of decoration on each side show that the vases were designed to be reversible. Josiah Wedgwood is known to have created variety in his London showroom displays by turning vases round every few days, in line with his intention that 'business, and amusement can be made to go hand in hand.'

[15] Lot 65

Lamp, about 1805

Haynes, Dillwyn & Co.

Pearlware

Height 24.2 cm, length 26.4 cm

Unmarked

Bequeathed by Ernest Morton Nance, 1952

NMW A 30807

The dark blue areas of this lamp were intended as the ground for a multi-coloured lustre called, according to William Dillwyn, 'Chamelion [sic], which exhibits the blended Colours of the Rainbow.' His son Lewis Weston, he continued, had 'been much engaged in the application of his Chemical Knowledge' to the development of 'his lustre.' The Cambrian Company sale catalogues of 1808 mention lustre more often than any other form of decoration, indicating that the Pottery's London warehouse was seen as a showcase for Lewis Weston's invention. As his father wrote, 'He intends [that] the public eye is dazzled by opening a shop in Fleet Street.'

A range of vases and other ornamental objects was designed for this lustre, but its shifting iridescent finish proved to be very fugitive and has now almost entirely disappeared. This range seems not to have sold very well, either. As George Haynes joked with dark humour in July 1807, 'The Lustre has been much admired but is dull of sale.'

This lamp is a Roman form and features a kneeling Vestal filling it at the top. It copies a Wedgwood design of about 1775, itself based on designs by the French amateur artist Jean-Claude-Richard de Saint-Non (1729-1791).

Honey pot, about 1805
Haynes, Dillwyn & Co.
Pearlware
Height 13.2 cm, diameter 14.2 cm
Mark: *SWANSEA*, impressed
Bequeathed by Ernest Morton Nance, 1952
NMW A 30735

Appropriately enough, this honey pot is in the form of a traditional skep beehive made from coils of straw. We can see a painted bee in its small entrance. Ceramic honey pots of this date are very rare, and must have been seen as novelty items. Wedgwood, Davenport and Elijah Mayer made skep honey pots in caneware at the beginning of the nineteenth century, but the significant differences in this pot's design suggest that Swansea looked elsewhere for inspiration. It may be that the source was silver honey pots of skep form, a number of which were made in the late 1790s and early 1800s by Paul Storr.

The decoration matches that of a cream jug and saucer in the Museum's collection, so they all could have been part of a breakfast set.

Supper set, about 1805
Haynes, Dillwyn & Co.
Pearlware
Central tureen: height 20.1 cm
Mark: *SWANSEA*, impressed
Bequeathed by Ernest Morton Nance, 1952
NMW A 30818-30835

Supper sets like this first appeared in the 1790s, an innovation related to the new practice of eating leftovers late at night. Production of properly fitting sets was expensive and demanded great precision, so only the more ambitious potteries like Swansea took the trouble to make them.

Swansea made supper sets in at least two configurations. The circular form has a central tureen surrounded by four quadrant-shaped dishes. This more elaborate oval design has an outer ring of narrow open dishes and two small, covered tureens, all designed to fit a large oval tray. Supper services typically came with a set of twelve plates.

Contemporary Dillwyn family letters highlight the novelty of such sets at the beginning of the nineteenth century and the confusion they could cause, even for the family of the proprietor. In 1804, William Dillwyn wrote to his daughter Suzanna in Philadelphia about a Swansea supper set sent to a relative in America, 'which he mentioned that he knew not how it was to be used – a difficulty which I hope [can be] removed by pointing out the necessity of a circular Mahogany Tray made to fit and contain the principle [*sic*] articles, forming a circle.'

Supper set with eight plates and tray, about 1805

Haynes, Dillwyn & Co.

Decorated by William Weston Young and Thomas Pardoe

Pearlware

Tray: diameter 53.4 cm
Tureen and cover: height 24 cm
Plates: diameter 20.3 cm

Mark: SWANSEA, impressed, on the five covers and several plates; C, impressed or incised on the five covers; incised numerals on the dishes and covers

Purchased with assistance from Art Fund, Dr Graham Jenkins and Jonathan Gray, 2015

NMW A 39578-39590, 51746

The comprehensive geographic spread of the animals painted on this supper set suggests an attempt to represent all the continents. From the Americas come the 'Panther' (a jaguar) and 'Striated Monkey' (common marmoset), from Europe the 'Chamois Goat' and 'Fallow Deer', from Asia the 'Ounce' (snow leopard) and 'Nylghau' (nilgai), from Africa the 'Zebra' and 'Lion', and from Australia the 'Kangaroo', possibly the earliest depiction of this animal on ceramics. Pride of place goes to the 'Tyger' in the bottom of the central tureen.[16]

The print sources used were predominantly George Shaw's *General Zoology*[17] and Thomas Bewick's *A General History of Quadrupeds*.[18] Other sources used may include Buffon's *Histoire Naturelle*[19] and engravings after George Stubbs's painting *The Kongouro from New Holland* (1772).

Those who first ate from this set may have been familiar with such exotic animals, which starred in the various menageries in London and travelling the country, and even roamed a number of Britain's country estates.

---

[16] Andrew Renton, 'A tabletop menagerie: a Cambrian Pottery zoological supper service', English Ceramic Circle Transactions, 27 (2016), pp. 119-141

[17] George Shaw, *General Zoology or Systematic Natural History: Mammalia*, vols 1 & 2 (1800, 1801)

[18] Thomas Bewick, *A General History of Quadrupeds* (1790)

[19] Georges-Louis Leclerc, Comte de Buffon, *Histoire Naturelle*, volume IX (1761) and later editions

Teapot, about 1805
Haynes, Dillwyn & Co.
Caneware
Height 7.8 cm, length 20.5 cm
Mark: *SWANSEA*, impressed
Bequeathed by Ernest Morton Nance, 1952
NMW A 30785

Joshua Gilpin, visiting the Cambrian Pottery in August 1796, mentioned the manufacture of 'The opaque yellow ware made to imitate pye crust, paste etc.' This is the unglazed stoneware body known as caneware, introduced by Wedgwood in the late 1770s and widely used from the mid-1780s until about 1820. It was used at the time to make game-pie dishes resembling pastry pie crusts, in response to flour shortages during the war with France. Swansea caneware is very rare. Other than a few game-pie dishes, the only known examples are this teapot, a matching cream jug now in the Royal Ontario Museum and a cream jug of a different design in the Victoria and Albert Museum.

The quality of the teapot, and the complexity of its moulded form, attest to the sophisticated modelling and mould-making skills at the Cambrian Pottery in the early nineteenth century. The shape is typical of teapots made around 1800-1810 by numerous firms, and derived from a fashionable classical style of teapot first made in silver and Sheffield plate.

The applied motifs in low relief depict a draped female figure pouring oil on a flaming brazier and another reading a book. Other manufacturers of the period used similar sprigs.

Cream tureen, about 1810-1812
Dillwyn & Co.
Pearlware
Height 14.4 cm, length 22.2 cm
Mark: *SWANSEA*, impressed
Purchased, 1926
NMW A 30778

This elegantly decorated cream tureen comes from a dessert service made around the time that Dillwyn's partnership with George Haynes ended, and management of the Cambrian Pottery switched to the new Bevington partnership. This tureen has the impressed S*WANSEA* mark thought to have been used between about 1804 and 1810, but other pieces with the same pattern bear the impressed mark *DILLWYN & Co* used in the years 1811-1817. The Cambrian Pottery clearly retained at least one skilled gilder following Thomas Pardoe's departure in 1809, and this pattern would not have been out of place on the Swansea porcelain produced from about 1815.

The shape includes an integral stand and is closely based on a Wedgwood design of about 1775. It is one of many Swansea shapes modelled on Wedgwood originals. Imitating Wedgwood's shapes and patterns was an important marketing ploy, a fact underlined by the many references to 'Wedgewood' wares in the 1808 sale catalogues of the Cambrian Warehouse.

Two plates, 1811-1817

Dillwyn & Co.

Pearlware

Left: diameter 25.2 cm, height 2.3 cm
Right: diameter 24.7 cm, height 2.4 cm

Mark: *DILLWYN & Co,* impressed

Bequeathed by Ernest Morton Nance, 1952

NMW A 31158 & 30664

These contrasting plates illustrate the shift in emphasis following the failure of the Cambrian Company venture in 1808 and the departures of chief painter Thomas Pardoe in 1809 and Dillwyn's partner George Haynes in 1810. Some hand-painting continued, but the primary focus now was on transfer-printed table wares.

Painting in underglaze colours probably stopped, but the plate on the left with its chinoiserie landscape shows that painting in underglaze blue persisted, sticking to a style typical of the 1780s. On-glaze enamelling was limited largely to a few patterns in bold Regency colours and botanical prints filled in by hand with enamel colours. From 1814, painted decoration saw a spectacular revival, but only on porcelain.

The printed plate has a pattern that appears to be unique to Swansea, featuring a leopard or cheetah stalking an antelope, also in a chinoiserie landscape. This was adapted from a tail-piece vignette in Thomas Bewick's *A General History of Quadrupeds*. Alongside distinctive patterns like this, the Pottery relied chiefly on common chinoiserie patterns such as a version of the Willow pattern known as the 'Long Bridge' pattern.

Engraved tail-piece to 'The Tiger' from Thomas Bewick, *A General History of Quadrupeds* (1790).

Figure group of two pointers, 1811-1817

Dillwyn & Co.

Feldspathic stoneware

Height 8 cm, length 13.6 cm

Mark: *DILLWYN & Co*, impressed

Purchased, 1988

NMW A 30740

The two dogs are the pointers Pluto and Juno, derived from an engraving used in 1802 in Reverend W. B. Daniels's *Rural Sports*. The figures are in low relief and have a flat back, an unusual type that is especially rare in a stoneware body.

The Cambrian Pottery made at least two different designs of this style of ornamental figure group on a stepped rectangular base. Another marked example features the figure of Toby Fillpot, best known in the form of toby jugs, seated at a table and smoking his pipe.

Given how rare they are, and that this ceramic body was not otherwise used at Swansea, it seems that this figure group was the result of a brief experiment. Perhaps this was the work of the J. W. Biggs from Coalport who, as the Swansea porcelain painter Henry Morris recalled in 1850, was employed at the Cambrian Pottery for a few months, probably in 1813, to make porcelain but had only 'succeeded in making a tolerable article in "Stonebody."'

Pluto and Juno, engraving by J. Scott after S. Gilpin, from Reverend W. B. Daniels, *Rural Sports* (1802). © The Trustees of the British Museum.

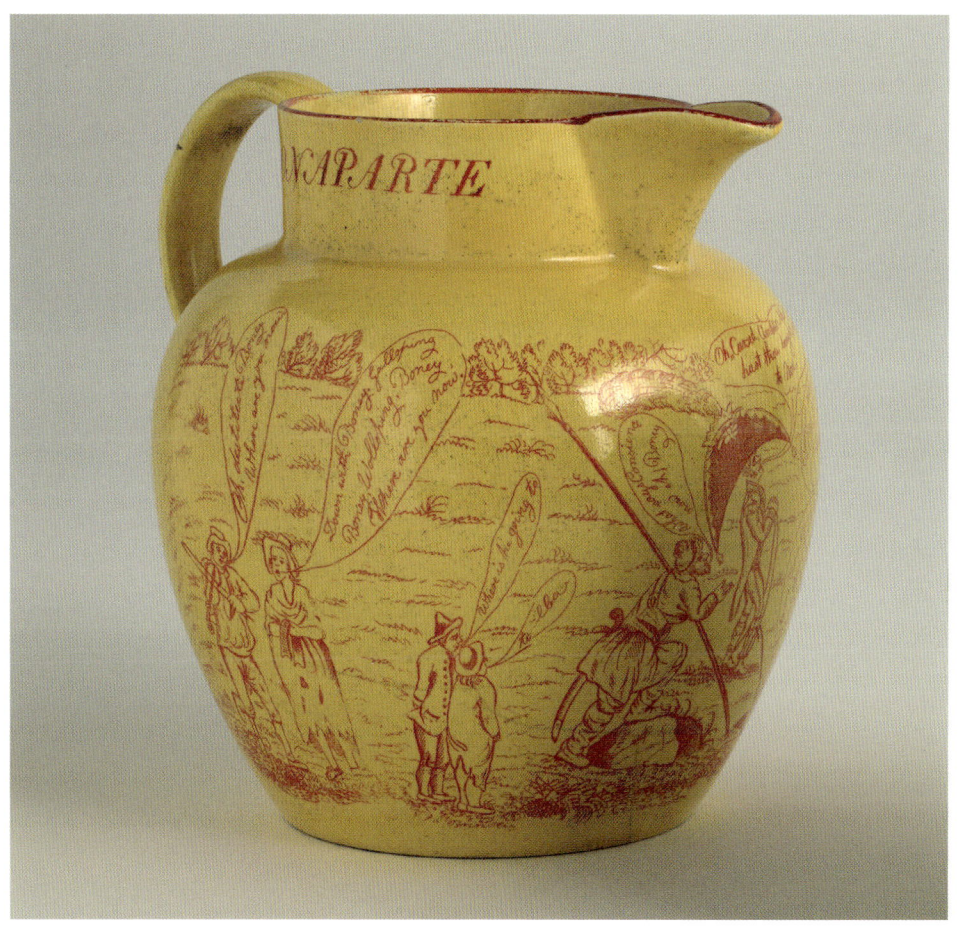

Jug, 1814
Dillwyn & Co.
Engraved by James Brindley
Yellow-glazed earthenware
Height 14 cm, diameter 13.2 cm
Unmarked; the print signed *Ja Brindley*
Bequeathed by Ernest Morton Nance, 1952
NMW A 30680

By 1813, perhaps knowing that Dillwyn was keen to explore porcelain manufacture, the engraver James Brindley came to Swansea from Staffordshire. He probably worked independently, repairing copper plates and engraving new patterns. Some of these appear on Swansea porcelain, but best known is this transfer print commemorating the defeat of Napoleon in April 1814 and his exile to the island of Elba.

This is a complex composition in the satirical tradition of James Gillray and Thomas Rowlandson. An inscription round the neck identifies the subject: *BONAPARTE DETHRON'D April 1st 1814,* altering the actual date by a few days to land on April Fool's Day. Printed in red, the image shows Napoleon in chains being dragged into a fiery pit by the Devil, and surrounded by various characters, all with speech bubbles. A man with an artificial leg and violin asks, 'Oh, destitute Boney / Where are you now'; while Bonaparte laments, 'Oh, Cursed Ambition what / hast thou brought me / to Now'; and the Devil says to him, 'Why to me Come. Come. / along thou hast been / a most Dutyful / Child.'

This engraving also appears on white earthenware jugs, printed in black and overpainted in enamels.

Cambrian Pottery jug with *BONAPARTE DETHRON'D* print, 1814.

The Heyday of the Cambrian Pottery 1789-1824

Jug, teapot and plate, about 1811-1817

Dillwyn & Co.

Earthenware

Jug: height 22.3 cm
Teapot: length 26 cm
Plate: diameter 20.5 cm

Mark: jug DILLWYN & Co. SWANSEA (printed in a circle); plate DILLWYN & Co (impressed)

Bequeathed by Ernest Morton Nance, 1952

NMW A 30670, 30704, 30691

These are examples of the good-quality printed earthenware produced at the Cambrian Pottery shortly before Lewis Weston Dillwyn began to make porcelain there. The beer jug celebrates Wellington's victories in Portugal and Spain between 1808 and 1812. It is printed in underglaze blue with Britannia in her chariot trampling the flag of France under her feet, and with a winged figure of Victory.

The pearlware teapot is printed in on-glaze brown with vignettes of shells and seaweed and with bands of leaves and flowers around the neck and cover. It probably celebrates a marriage, being inscribed *Thomas Cornish to Mary Northey, June 30th, 1813*. The only Thomas and Mary so far found at this date were from Gwennap, a copper mining district in Cornwall, and they soon went on to marry other partners.

The Cambrian Pottery also made sets of creamware dessert plates, printed in black or a red-brown with birds and feathers after woodcuts by the great Newcastle engraver Thomas Bewick (1753-1828). Shown here is the female little bittern from Bewick's *Water Birds* of 1804.

4 | The Swansea China Works 1814-1826

In March 1810 the Dillwyn and Haynes partnership was dissolved. Dillwyn promptly invested in new buildings and equipment, nearly doubling the Pottery's output, and the following year he took his manager Timothy Bevington and his son John into a limited partnership. Thomas Pardoe had also left to establish his own china- and glass-decorating business in Bristol, but the factory introduced a new range of fine printed earthenwares, and was making a profit of £1,500-£2,000 a year in 1810-1813. Despite the closure in 1808 of the short-lived Cambrian Company in London, Dillwyn retained an ambition to make fine wares for the London market. To do so, he had to produce porcelains that could compete with the leading English factories and with French imports. There is evidence that Swansea made a small quantity of porcelain around 1806, and trials may have resumed in 1813.

Quite independently, William Billingsley (see p. 139) and Samuel Walker had arrived at Nantgarw in November of that year. They had been working for the Worcester firm of Barr, Flight and Barr, where they had developed a new porcelain body. However, it was not put into production, and they left hurriedly with the intention of producing it themselves.

By the summer of 1814, they had evolved an exceptionally translucent porcelain at Nantgarw. This was a glassy fritted body comprising bone ash, sand and potash mixed with china clay, but it was difficult to work and kiln losses were high. They soon exhausted their small capital, and in September 1814 they agreed to come to Swansea, where Dillwyn would build the Swansea China Works, adjoining the Cambrian Pottery. He soon concluded that the Nantgarw body 'was too nearly allied to glass to bear the necessary heat.' It took a year to perfect a porcelain kiln, and to develop alternative bodies, but by the autumn of 1815 they were selling small quantities of porcelain locally.

The factory produced two quite different types of porcelain – fritted bodies containing soapstone, which have a granular appearance and at times a near white translucency (not unlike French hard-paste porcelain), and a mixed body of china clay, china stone and bone ash, similar to the bone china that was becoming the standard recipe in British porcelain factories. The latter also contained varying amounts of blue clay and lime, which produced a slight greenish tinge and led to it being known as the 'duck-egg' body.

In July 1816 the factory celebrated the acquisition of a tea service by the Prince Regent's daughter, Princess Charlotte, and the new porcelains were launched on the London market. Rather than opening another showroom, the factory sold its porcelain through the leading independent retailers of the day, especially Mortlock's in Oxford Street. In order to appeal to a sophisticated metropolitan market, Swansea modelled its wares closely on contemporary French porcelain. It employed a French gilder and developed an outstanding team of china painters. Several of these, notably David Evans, Henry Morris and William Pollard, specialised in arrangements of wild and garden flowers. Thomas Baxter (see p. 140), who had trained as an artist in the Royal Academy Schools, also worked for the factory in 1816-1819, while part of its production was supplied 'in the white' (unpainted) to independent decorators. These wares duly attracted the rich and fashionable. In September 1817 *The Cambrian* reported that 'the magnificent services of porcelain now executing by the Cambrian Manufactory for the Marquesses of Bute and Exeter, and Mr Coutts far excel any china we have seen manufactured in this country.'

Nevertheless, much Swansea porcelain, especially tea services, was not decorated with free-hand painting, but with simple repeating or 'set' patterns that could be produced quickly by semi-skilled workers. These wares competed for a middle-class market with those of many other factories, during a period of economic depression. Although the bone china body was a beautiful porcelain, another fritted body with a high soapstone content was introduced in March 1817. This has a distinct yellowish translucency and a slightly pitted glaze. It is known as 'trident', from the impressed mark it often bears. Despite these shortcomings, Dillwyn was convinced that the factory was on the brink of financial success; but in September 1817 his father-in-law died, leaving him with the responsibility of running the estate left to his then underage son. He leased the Cambrian Pottery and the Swansea China Works to a new partnership led by John and Timothy Bevington, and sold the (mostly undecorated) stock for £2,500. Although the Bevington partnership made very little porcelain after 1817, it had thousands of pieces painted for sale until January 1826.

Teacup and saucer, 1815-1816
Perhaps painted by William Billingsley
Soapstone porcelain[20]
Cup: height 6.5 cm
Saucer: diameter 13.9 cm
Mark: Swansea painted in gold (saucer)
Given by Hubert Alexander, 1924
NMW A 31129

These are made of a very white, slightly grainy porcelain body containing a small quantity of soaprock. This was developed in Swansea through a series of experiments during 1815, and was intended to look like the hard-paste French porcelains popular with wealthy British customers. Dillwyn wrote of making 'two species of china resembling foreign china', and the factory also employed a French gilder.

William Billingsley presumably had some involvement in these trials, but he was initially responsible for decorating the new china. He had trained as an enameller, and by the 1780s had been the Derby factory's leading flower painter. Dillwyn writes in September 1815 of a 25-guinea vase 'which Beeley painted' (Billingsley later took the name Beeley, see p. 139) and the Swansea painter Henry Morris recalled in 1850 that decoration at the factory was 'executed by, or under the direction of Mr Bailey.'

Distinguishing Billingsley's work from that of the painters he supervised is difficult; however, this cup and saucer, superlatively painted with a band of garden flowers (including his 'signature' roses), may be an example.

[20] See p. 47 for the different types of porcelain made at Swansea. Pieces discussed here have been identified visually rather than by chemical analysis. Although porcelain was produced commercially from the autumn of 1815, it is assumed here that nearly all Swansea porcelain was formed and fired in 1816 and 1817. This stock continued to be decorated locally until about 1825

Cream tureen, 1816-1824[21]

Painted by David Evans

Soapstone porcelain

Height 18.5 cm

Mark: Swansea painted in purple

Purchased, 1992 (Sir Leslie Joseph Collection)

NMW A 31079

There were usually two of these vessels in a standard twenty-four plate dessert service, and they were used for the creams or fruit sauces that were served with dessert. Most cream tureens have a circular stand, but this one is supported on three lion's paw feet. It is another example of the factory's familiarity with contemporary French design. The design originated in Paris around 1800, and it is described in the 1820 shape book of the Spode factory, which also copied it, as a 'round French cream bowl on three claws – three heads on each'. The porcelain body appears to be the soapstone-rich 'trident' porcelain introduced in the spring of 1817. The tureen is lavishly gilded, and it was painted by David Evans with a wreath of naturalistic garden flowers including morning glory, pink roses, a purple and yellow tulip and bluebells.

---

[21] In this chapter objects are given a date range that represents the earliest likely date of the manufacture of the porcelain body and the latest possible date of the decoration (David Evans left Swansea in 1824)

Two cabinet cups and saucers, 1816-1825
Probably painted by George Beddow
Bone porcelain
Cups: height 12.4 cm
Saucers: diameter 15.5 cm
Unmarked
Purchased, 1992 (Sir Leslie Joseph Collection), and given by the Friends of Amgueddfa Cymru, 1996
NMW A 31073 & 32641

Sometimes called chocolate cups, these paw-footed vessels were another French-inspired shape. Originally intended for the London market, they are largely ornamental and often lavishly decorated. The landscapes within the rich blue and gold grounds may be the work of George Beddow, who was working in Swansea as a ceramic painter specialising in landscapes prior to 1814, and remained in the employ of the Bevingtons until 1826. The scene on the cup on the left is *Tenby from / the / Hotel* and its saucer has *Pembroke Dock Yard / from West Lanion PILL*. These are taken from a set of coloured aquatints by the Tenby artist Charles Norris (1779-1858), published in Pembroke in 1820 and seen on other Swansea cabinet cups of this type. The cup on the right, however, is painted with Conwy Castle, while its saucer is titled 'view in Italy'.

Plate, 1816

Perhaps painted by David Evans

Bone porcelain

Diameter 21.4 cm

Unmarked

James Pyke Thompson collection. Transferred from Turner House, 1921

NMW A 30127

The plate has a cruciform moulding. The centre is painted with a spray of pink and white briar roses, and the border with a wreath of wildflowers including wild strawberries, speedwell, red campion, Michaelmas daisy and bluebells. There is no gilding to distract from the effect of the flowers against the white porcelain body.

It was once part of a dessert service known as the Dynevor service. This may perhaps be the 'Dessert Service China Wild Flowers' bought by the Carmarthenshire landowner George Talbot Rice, 3rd Lord Dynevor (1765-1852), for the large sum of £88 4s in June 1816. The decorator may be David Evans (about 1795-1881), who is first recorded in Swansea in March of that year. He remained at the factory until about 1824 when he went to work as a flower painter for the firm of Grainger, Lee & Co. in Worcester.

Teapot and stand, sugar bowl and cup and saucer, 1816-1825

Bone porcelain

Teapot: height 12.9 cm
Saucer: diameter 15.2 cm

Mark: SWANSEA printed in red

Bequeathed by Ernest Morton Nance, 1952

NMW A 30936, 30937 and 30935

Teawares of this flattened oval shape are rare in British porcelain of the early nineteenth century, although similar shallow fluted cups were made in France, probably from around 1810. At Swansea they are generally decorated with gilding only (most enamelled pieces seem to be later-decorated). An advertisement for the final sale of the factory's stock in January 1826 mentions a 'very handsome complete Breakfast service, Paris fluted, broad gold bands', which probably describes pieces of this sort.

The factory also made small plates and muffin dishes of this design. The cups are found in different sizes, and with both kidney-scroll (as here) and loop handles. The teapot and sugar bowl here are moulded with concave flutes, while a more upright variant has convex flutes and a kidney-scroll handle. The cup and saucer are more elaborately decorated with a band of scallop shells, and personalised with a boar's head crest.

Group of vases, 1816-1825

Large vase: soapstone porcelain.
Others: bone porcelain

Maximum height 26.1 cm

Mark: various Swansea

Bequeathed by Ernest Morton Nance, 1952; purchased, 1913; purchased, 1988

NMW A 30889, 30900, 30901, 30910, 30911 and 30919

To cater for a growing taste among the wealthy for ornamental objects around the house, the Swansea China Works made at least a dozen different vase forms as well as decorative match pots, inkwells, pen trays and candlesticks. The largest of the vases shown here, with its fan and anthemion handles, is a copy of a contemporary French design. Made in two sections bolted together by a brass rod, it was painted outside the factory with romantic landscapes, possibly for the London retailer Pellatt & Green.

The others are all painted with the garden flowers that were one of the factory's specialities. The pair of slender trumpet vases has warped in the kiln and may be a unique survival. The smaller egg-shaped vases with bee handles were more successful and the design was also made with a pedestal base. The last of the group – with eagle handles – was made in two sizes and with other minor variations.

Wine cooler, 1816-1822
Probably painted by William Pollard
Bone porcelain
Height 17.2 cm, diameter 20.6 cm
Mark: SWANSEA printed in red
Purchased, 1948
NMW A 31153

This is one of a pair of wine coolers or ice pails. It is extremely rare, as all the porcelain mixes used at the factory prioritised the whiteness of the paste over its plasticity, making it difficult to produce pieces as large as this. Customers may also have felt that silver or Sheffield plate bottle coolers would be more robust, and visually impressive, than porcelain ones.

It is painted with a frieze of garden and wildflowers above an elaborately gilded foot. The enameller is thought to have been William Pollard, who was born in Swansea in 1803. He left in 1822 to work at Henry Daniel's factory in Stoke-on-Trent, where a number of patterns feature his distinctive 'Burrows' rose and other wildflowers. This magnificent example of his mature style is therefore unlikely to be earlier than 1820. He returned to south Wales in 1827 to work as a china decorator and retailer in Carmarthen and later in Swansea.

Cabaret tea service, 1816-1819

Painted by Thomas Baxter

Bone porcelain

Teapot: height 12.8 cm
Tray: width 31.7 cm

Marks: SWANSEA impressed on the tray; other pieces Swansea painted in purple

Purchased, 1986; the cup and saucer lent anonymously

NMW A 31132-31136; NMW A (L) 518

This is a breakfast tea service for two people (one cup and saucer is missing). Known today as a cabaret service, these were intended as much for ornament as for use. In the early nineteenth century, they were more usually called 'dejeunes' (after the French *déjeuner*), and in July 1816 the *Morning Chronicle* reported that 'a new manufactory has been established in Wales, the brilliancy of the white and the transparency being equal to the celebrated Porcelaine of the Royal Sèvres Manufactory. We understand Her Royal Highness the Princess Charlotte and Princess Mary have each a superb dejeune of the Cambrian Porcelaine.'

Swansea made several designs for such services. This one was painted by Thomas Baxter (see p. 140), with monochrome cupids at play, in his soft stippled manner. The simple wave-scroll gilding also seems particular to Baxter and emphasises the whiteness of the body.

Plate, 1816-1819

Painted by Thomas Baxter

Bone porcelain

Diameter 21.5 cm

Mark: Swansea painted in grey

Accepted by HM Government in lieu of tax and allocated to Amgueddfa Cymru 2006

NMW A 38267

This plate was probably intended for display rather than use, as it does not seem to be part of a service. The centre is exquisitely enamelled with a group of shells on a marble slab. These may have been painted from real examples in Baxter's possession, rather than from engravings such as the illustrations to Lewis Weston Dillwyn's own *Descriptive Catalogue of Recent Shells* (1817). Baxter painted an almost identical composition of shells on a cabinet plate for the Chamberlain factory, following his departure in 1819 for Worcester, where he died in April 1821.

Shell painting is found on some of the best British and European porcelain of the day. It enabled the painter to demonstrate a very high level of skill, and it associated the patron with the newly discovered wonders of the natural world, which also found expression in the fashionable hobby of collecting exotic shells.

Two plates, 1816-1819

Painted by Thomas Baxter

Bone porcelain

Left: diameter 21 cm
Right: diameter 21.7 cm

Mark: left Swansea painted in black; right SWANSEA impressed

Bequeathed by Ernest Morton Nance, 1952. Purchased, 1992 (Sir Leslie Joseph Collection)

NMW A 31138 & 31074

The right-hand plate, painted with marigolds and anemones, forms part of a service made for Lewis Weston Dillwyn, described on completion in September 1817 as 'the china dessert service painted with garden scenery by Mr. Baxter'. With the exception of this plate and another in the Victoria and Albert Museum, this service remains in the possession of his descendants. Some of the scenes – all unique – depicted on its forty-one pieces may be views in the grounds at Penllergaer, his wife's family home, but most are probably imaginative.

The large arrangements of flowers against a distant landscape are unusual and may have been inspired by engravings after Philip Reinagle in Robert Thornton's *Temple of Flora*, published from 1798 to 1807. The plate on the left, with its gilt anthemion border, is also painted by Baxter with a similar subject – a marble urn overflowing with flowers and foliage, including pink roses and yellow narcissus.

Soup tureen, cream tureen and vegetable dish, 1816-about 1820

Swansea China Works

Decorated outside the factory, probably in London

Bone porcelain

Soup tureen: height 25.5 cm
Cream tureen: height 13.7 cm
Dish: height 16.5 cm

Mark: SWANSEA impressed on the vegetable dish and cream tureen stand

Bequeathed by David Lewis, 1994

NMW A 32281, 32284 and 32289

These are just three examples from a lavishly decorated dinner and dessert service, made in Swansea's mixed bone body, which has a slight greenish tinge. Comprising around 250 pieces, this service is now scattered across many collections. It was first recorded in 1922, when it was sold at Christie's from the estate of the great Victorian philanthropist Angela, Baroness Burdett-Coutts (1814-1906). It may therefore have been commissioned by her grandfather, the banker Thomas Coutts (1735-1822), perhaps at the time of his second marriage to the actress Harriet Mellon in 1816. According to *The Cambrian*, reporting on 20 September 1817, one of three 'magnificent services of porcelain now executing by the Cambrian Manufactory' was destined for 'Mr Coutts'.

The whole service is richly painted with baskets of garden flowers, on a background of grass and flowering plants, and sprays of pink roses. The enamelling and gilding are the work of an independent decorating business, possibly that of the Sims family in Pimlico, London.

Angela Burdett-Coutts, chromolithograph by Théobald Chartran, published in *Vanity Fair*, 1883.
© National Portrait Gallery, London.

The Swansea China Works 1814-1826

Cabaret tea service, 1816-about 1820

Decorated outside the factory, probably in London

Bone porcelain

Teapot: height 13 cm
Jug: height 11 cm
Sugar bowl: height 12 cm
Slop bowl: height 7.7 cm
Cup: height 8.8 cm
Tray: length 47.6 cm

Mark: DILLWYN & CO / SWANSEA impressed above crossed tridents (tray)

Given by W. S. de Winton, 1918

NMW A 30119-30124

This breakfast tea service is at the height of Regency fashion. The upright pieces are in the form of neo-classical urns, and the borders are moulded with acanthus leaves. It must have been very difficult to fire without damage in the kiln and, not surprisingly, it is one of Swansea's rarest designs.

It has an unusual impressed mark, and was probably a special commission. As with other orders of this sort, the rich decoration of rose sprays was added outside the factory, perhaps in the Sims enamelling and gilding workshop in London. The service forms part of the great collection of British and European porcelain W. S. de Winton assembled between the 1890s and the 1920s.

Square dish, centre dish, ice cream pail and base, plate and cream tureen, 1816-1817

Decorated outside the factory, probably in London

Bone porcelain

Square dish: length 24.4 cm
Centre dish: length 36.2 cm
Pail: height 18.9 cm
Base: diameter 23.7 cm
Plate: diameter 23.7 cm
Tureen: height 14.1 cm

Mark: SWANSEA impressed (centre dish, square dish, plates)

Purchased with the assistance of the Art Fund, 1998

NMW A 33713, 33712, 33709, 33727, 33728 & 33710

These pieces form part of a large dessert service made for Brownlow Cecil, 2nd Marquess of Exeter (1795-1867). Each piece bears brightly painted flowers amid grasses and with bands of hatched and shaded gilding, comprising fluted vases with conical covers alternating with arabesques, floriate scrolls and florets. The boat-shaped centre dish has a large red and cream tulip amid fly honeysuckle and the square dish (one of four) a pink and white anemone amid gypsophila. The pail (one of two in the service) bears honeysuckle on one side and a passionflower on the other. The plate has scarlet poppies with buttercups and forget-me-nots. The cream or sugar tureen is painted on one side with maroon and yellow primula and on the other with pink and white aquilegia, and its stand bears red fuchsia. Each flower is accurately reproduced, probably from botanical prints, but made less formal by the addition of grasses.

The service was still in production in September 1817. The decoration (also found on a similar service formerly at Gosford Castle, County Armagh) is of the highest quality and was probably commissioned by the factory from a London enameller.

Brownlow Cecil, 2nd Marquess of Exeter, after James Sant stipple engraving, 1844.
© National Portrait Gallery, London.

Centre dish, 1816-about 1825
Decorated by John and James Bradley, London
Bone porcelain
Height 13 cm, diameter 26.7 cm
Unmarked
Bequeathed by David Lewis, 1994
NMW A 32336

The dish, the centrepiece of a dessert service, is painted with exotic birds copied from hand-coloured engravings in George Edwards *A Natural History of Uncommon Birds,* 1750. The interior bears a Horned Indian Pheasant. Edwards had only a drawing to work from. He wrote 'The Tail appeared in the original Draught, a little brushy at the End, as if broken off by being kept in a Cage or Coop: It was in length the proportion that I have here given it, but I imagine that this most rare and curious Bird, in the Perfection has the Tail something, if not a great Deal longer: so that I have left it doubtful by casting it behind a tree.' On the outside of the bowl are the equally rare Greater American Godwit and the Demoiselle of Numidia.

Some pieces from this, or a similar service, are inscribed *J. Bradley & Co, 47 Pall Mall, London*. John Bradley took a house in Pall Mall in 1812, described in directories as a 'china' or Coalbrookdale warehouse. He was also a painter in enamels, exhibiting regularly at the Royal Academy from 1817. A writer in *The Pottery Gazette* in 1885 remembered how John and James Bradley 'brought the art of china decorating to London, and taught it to the aristocracy...' The address 47 Pall Mall probably dates the decoration of these pieces to after 1821, as the house, previously 54, was renumbered in that year.

Horned Indian Pheasant from George Edwards, *A Natural History of Uncommon Birds.*

Plate, 1816-about 1825
Probably decorated by John Powell, London
Bone porcelain
Diameter 21.7cm
Mark: SWANSEA impressed
Given by the Cardiff Exhibition Committee, 1882
NMW A 31286

This plate was probably decorated by the London enameller and china dealer John Powell, whose studio was at 91 Wimpole Street. The centre is painted with Ariadne on the shores of Naxos accompanied by a tearful cherub and an angel who points towards a ship bearing away her faithless lover Theseus. The source of this Classical scene is a Roman wall painting discovered in 1757 at Pompeii.

This was transferred to the Royal Collection of antiquities in Naples (now the National Archaeological Museum). It was published in the series *Antichita d'Ercolano* in 1760 and was known through other engravings by the time the plate was produced.

Sugar box and cover, 1817-about 1825

Decorated outside the factory, probably in London

Soapstone porcelain

Length 14.8 cm

Mark: SWANSEA and a trident impressed; Pellatt & Green, / LONDON. printed in red

Given by F. E. Andrews, 1921

NMW A 31308

The Swansea China Works advertised in 1817 that their porcelains could be obtained from four major London retailers, including Pellatt and Green 'Potters and Glass Manufacturers to the King' at 6, St Paul's Churchyard.

One of the factory's aims was to produce a porcelain that closely resembled imported French hard-paste porcelain, and the Swansea soapstone body at its best had the same whiteness and grainy feel. This sugar box was decorated by or for Pellatt and Green and forms part of a tea service that otherwise comprises Paris porcelain pieces. This is decorated with gilt stems and foliage, and with blue and purple flower heads in low-fired enamels added after the gilding in the French manner.

Pellatt and Green's showroom. Aquatint from Ackermann's *Repository of the Arts*, 1, 1809.

Pair of vases, 1817-about 1820
Decorated outside the factory, probably in London
Soapstone porcelain
Height 14.5 cm
Mark: SWANSEA impressed, a trident below. Reserves signed 'Oldfield'
Purchased, 2003
NMW A 37151-37152

The shape, with its ram's-head handles, is French in origin and made by several British factories. The body is the soapstone-rich trident paste introduced at Swansea in 1817, although the translucency of these vases is better than most of the Swansea trident porcelain.

They were decorated outside the factory, possibly by John Edwin Oldfield, a London artist who mostly made topographical watercolours, but also painted literary subjects on porcelain. His subject here is 'Crazy Kate' from William Cowper's poem *The Task* (1785): 'A serving-maid was she, who fell in love With one who left her, went to sea, and died...' One vase depicts the love-struck Kate in a flowery garden. On the other, bereft and in rags, she 'roams the dreary waste'.

Pair of spill vases, 1816-1819
Decorated outside the factory
Bone porcelain
Height 11.4 cm
Mark: 'MM / SWANSEA / 1819' painted in red enamel
Purchased, 1992 (Sir Leslie Joseph Collection)
NMW A 31077-31078

These vases are painted with animals and birds in imitation of Chinese porcelain of the early eighteenth century. Although the decoration is competent, the inscription suggests that it was probably the work of an amateur. Painting in enamels was a socially acceptable pastime for women of leisure in the early nineteenth century, though they needed access to a muffle kiln to fire their work. 'MM' is traditionally identified as Mary Moggridge, although she has not been identified with any certainty.

The Moggridges were south Wales landowners and industrialists, and a branch of the family lived in Swansea. Lewis Weston Dillwyn's daughter Fanny later married Matthew Moggridge.

Pieces from a tea service, 1816-about 1825

Bone porcelain

Teapot: height 15 cm, length 26.5 cm

Mark: SWANSEA printed in red (plate); 219 painted in red on several pieces

Given by Vernon Thorne, 1995

NMW A 32558-32563, and 32573

These pieces form part of a complete tea service in the collection, which is made up of a teapot and stand, a waste bowl, a cream jug, a sugar box, a plate, twelve teacups and saucers and twelve coffee cups. Versions of the boxy-shaped teapot were made by many British factories, and the design was called the 'London' shape at Spode where it was introduced around 1813.

The service is painted with a brightly-coloured design inspired by Japanese Imari porcelain, comprising a central rock, flower and fence motif, and an underglaze blue border decorated with chrysanthemums and gilt foliage with three oval reserves of naturalistic flowers. It bears the pattern number 219.

Most Swansea porcelains, especially teawares, were decorated with conventional repeating patterns of this sort, rather than with the flower painting particularly associated with the Swansea China Works. The factory's pattern book does not survive, but over one hundred and fifty of these 'set' or repeating patterns are known, and this was perhaps the most popular.

Tankard, mug and dessert dish, 1816-about 1825

Bone porcelain

Tankard: height 16.8 cm

Mug: height 9.8 cm

Dish: length 28.2 cm

Mark: SWANSEA printed in red

Tankard bequeathed by Ernest Morton Nance, 1952
NMW A 30986

Mug bequeathed by Canon H. F. B. Mackay, 1936
NMW A 30981

Dish, purchased, 1986
NMW A 30991

All three pieces are decorated with an on-glaze black transfer-print of figures in an oriental landscape, overpainted in enamels. This decoration is known as 'the Mandarin' pattern and one example with the pattern number 164 is known. Several other British factories of the period made similar chinoiserie designs, which are derived from late-eighteenth-century Chinese export porcelain.

The tankard and the mug are both rare forms; the dish comes from a dessert service made for Thomas Lloyd (1788-1845) of Bronwydd, Cardiganshire, probably on the occasion of his marriage to Anne Davies of Llwydcoed, Llanon, Carmarthenshire, on 23 July 1819, and bears his crest and motto.

Two plates, 1816-about 1825

Bone porcelain

Left: diameter 20.9 cm

Right: diameter 21.1 cm

Mark: SWANSEA in red script

Purchased, 1992 (Sir Leslie Joseph Collection)

NMW A 31085 & 31086

Both plates are decorated with stylised floral patterns in a bright enamel palette, and one might almost think that they date from the 1920s rather than the 1820s. Although neither has a painted pattern number, they are examples of the factory's 'set' patterns, used primarily on teawares.

The design on the plate on the left is based on the convolvulus tricolor, a species of morning glory native to the Mediterranean. The plate on the right is painted with a 'Japan' pattern of chrysanthemum and lilies. Both were previously in the possession of Sir Leslie Joseph (1908-1992), who assembled an exceptional collection of Welsh ceramics between the 1950s and 1990.

Soup tureen, stand and ladle, 1817-1822

Bone porcelain (ladle: earthenware)

Height 25.6 cm, diameter 39.8 cm

Mark: BEVINGTON & CO and SWANSEA impressed (on stand)

Given by Miss Freda Gibbins, 1965

NMW A 31262 and 31263

Although the partnership led by John and Timothy Bevington was later to claim that the porcelain recipes they had received from Lewis Weston Dillwyn were useless to them, the Bevingtons appear to have made some attempt to manufacture further stocks of porcelain between September 1817 and September 1822, when they surrendered their lease of the China Works. Nevertheless, pieces with a 'BEVINGTON & CO' mark are extremely rare.

This tureen and stand form part of a dinner service made in porcelain for a member of the Bevington family. The paste is quite grainy and yellow in colour, but seems to be a mixed, bone china-like body. The ladle is made of earthenware. The service is printed in underglaze blue with an Italianate landscape pattern, known as the 'Castle', introduced at Spode around 1806 and copied by a number of other British factories. It was also used on earthenware at Swansea.

Punch-bowl, 1817-1825

Probably Swansea China Works

Perhaps bone porcelain

Height 17.7 cm, diameter 36.2 cm

Unmarked. Inscribed *this Bowl is respectfully / presented to the Corporation / of / LLWCHWR / by / JOHN BEVINGTON / of Swansea / January 1st 182*5

Given anonymously, 2021

NMW A 39697

John Bevington presented this bowl to the Corporation of Llwchwr (Lougher in English) on the western side of Swansea in January 1825. He and his father Timothy had given up the China Works in September 1822, while retaining the stock. Unless it was obtained 'in the white' from another manufacturer, this bowl is one of the rare pieces of porcelain actually made by the Bevingtons. It was decorated by one of the Swansea china painters, probably Henry Morris, with bouquets of flowers together with the arms of Llwchwr (including the ravens of the 6th-century king Urien Rheged) and the leeks and dragons of Wales.

Between September 1822 and January 1826 Swansea porcelain was fired at the Hafod Pipe Works and later at the Cambrian Brewery, other businesses in the town in which the Bevingtons had a stake.

5 | The Nantgarw China Works 1813-1814 and 1816-1823

The wares of this small Welsh factory were made right at the end of many decades of experimentation, in which British porcelain makers developed a bewildering variety of experimental pastes. Nantgarw porcelains are a fritted (ground) body including bone ash, sand and potash mixed with china clay, and they have a beauty and individuality that is lacking in the bone china wares that were rapidly becoming universal in the industry at the time.

When still in his twenties, the enameller William Billingsley (1758-1828) became the principal painter of flowers at the Derby porcelain factory. However, he devoted much of his life to an ultimately unsuccessful attempt to produce a white, translucent porcelain body that would surpass both imported European wares and those of the leading English factories of the day. Having failed to do this on a commercial scale, first at Pinxton in Derbyshire (1796-1799) and then at Brampton-in-Torksey in Lincolnshire (1803-1808), Billingsley and his son-in-law and collaborator Samuel Walker had since been employed by the Worcester firm of Barr, Flight and Barr (1808-1813). There, they developed another highly translucent soft-paste porcelain body. But it was not put into production, and they left Worcester hurriedly with the intention of producing it themselves.

Late in 1813 they came to Nantgarw, seven miles north of Cardiff. With the help of William Weston Young, who had worked as a pottery painter in Swansea, they rented a house on the bank of the Glamorganshire canal. In March 1814 one visitor, the Welsh visionary and antiquarian Iolo Morganwg, saw their earliest wares and wrote that he 'was shown some specimins of the real China brought from China, of the Dresden porcelane, of the French, hitherto the finest in the world. The Worcester, Burslem, Bristol etc. but tho' all of them very fine, they are greatly inferior in fineness to the Ware of Nant Garw'.

Though indeed beautiful, their glassy fritted paste was insufficiently plastic, and many pieces collapsed in the kiln. In September 1814 they sought help from the Board of Trade, claiming that their porcelain was as good as the French porcelain currently imported 'in the white' and hinting that further improvements would enable them to combine the 'whiteness and semi-transparency' of the best French porcelain 'with the firmness and closeness of Grain peculiar to the Saxon or Dresden.' No government help was forthcoming, but Lewis Weston Dillwyn, the proprietor of the Cambrian Pottery, agreed with them that they should make porcelain for him in Swansea, where he built the Swansea China Works. He soon concluded that the Nantgarw porcelain paste was not commercially viable, and instead developed alternatives.

After a couple of years in Swansea, Billingsley and Walker returned to Nantgarw, having managed to raise enough additional capital from Young and other shareholders to re-open and expand their small factory. Nantgarw porcelain arrived on the London market in early 1818. There, it was sold 'in the white' and decorated by a number of metropolitan enamelling and gilding businesses. Its lustrous glaze and highly translucent body were widely admired, and John Mortlock of Oxford Street was one of a number of major London retailers to sell lavishly decorated Nantgarw porcelains to an elite market. Despite this success, kiln losses remained high, and the factory still lost money. Early in 1820 Billingsley and Walker abandoned Nantgarw and went to work at the Coalport factory. William Weston Young was left with a stock of white porcelain, some of it unglazed. In order to salvage something from the disaster, he persuaded his friend Thomas Pardoe, then working as a china painter in Bristol, to come to Nantgarw, where with the help of a small number of relatively unskilled helpers, he decorated the remaining stock for sale locally. The last sale by auction of decorated and undecorated wares took place in October 1822, though Thomas Pardoe may have continued with some work at Nantgarw until his death in July 1823. His son William Henry Pardoe began to manufacture stoneware bottles and brown-glazed earthenwares at Nantgarw in 1833. The business, which also made clay pipes, continued under his descendants until its closure in 1920, and the factory site is now the Nantgarw Chinaworks Museum.

In 1832 Dionysius Lardner noted in *The Cabinet of Useful Arts*, 'since the discontinuance of this establishment, the excellent quality of its ware has been more justly estimated, and the prices now eagerly given by amateurs and collectors for pieces of Nungarrow porcelain, are out of all proportion greater than were originally demanded by the makers.'

Tumbler, 1818-1819
Perhaps gilded by William Billingsley
Frit porcelain
Height 7.6 cm
Unmarked
Given by Allan E. Renwick, 1938
NMW A 31249

The square and compass are an emblem of Freemasonry, and the conjoined sun and moon (on the reverse) are also associated with the masons. It may be one of the '6 Tumblers in Masonic Emblems' bought from the Nantgarw Porcelain Manufactory by Mr Hopkin Jones on 20 August 1819. These cost £1 7s, or 4/6 each. Mr Hopkin Jones was probably the landlord of the Globe Inn, Neath, who died in 1830. Very little porcelain was decorated and sold locally from Nantgarw during the second and main production period (1818 to early 1820), as Billingsley and Walker were supplying as much as they could to the London china trade 'in the white'.

Handwritten bill for six Masonic tumblers, annotated as balanced by William Beeley (as Billingsley called himself at this time) on 4 December 1819.

Pieces from a tea service, 1818-1820

Decorated outside the factory, probably in London

Frit porcelain

Teapot: length 24.1 cm
Sugar box: length 17.4 cm
Jug: length 15.5 cm
Bowl: diameter 17.4 cm
Plate: diameter 24 cm
Cups: height 7.2 cm

Mark: NANT-GARW CW impressed (plate only)

Bequeathed by David Lewis, 1994

NMW A 32290-32293, 32295 & 32299, 32302, 32306

The white porcelains made at Nantgarw were highly prized on the London retail market. These pieces form part of a large tea and coffee service decorated there for one of King George III's children. It is said to have been made for the marriage of Princess Mary (1776-1857) to her cousin William Frederick (1776-1834), Duke of Gloucester, in July 1816. However, the service was sold at Christie's on the death of Princess Mary's nephew, the 2nd Duke of Cambridge, in 1904, so its first owner may have been the King's youngest son Prince Adolphus (1774-1850), Duke of Cambridge, who married Augusta of Hesse-Cassel in June 1818, when Nantgarw porcelain was becoming available for decoration in London.

The unusual round shapes are derived from contemporary Paris porcelain. Also French in inspiration is the unevenly applied blue-green ground ornamented with an *oeil de perdrix* pattern (reserves of gilt spots within a border of blue dots), reserved with oval panels painted with roses and garden flowers. The shallow cups are for tea and the more upright ones are for coffee.

Cabinet Cup and Saucer, 1818-1820

Decorated outside the factory, probably in London

Frit porcelain

Cup: height 10 cm
Saucer: diameter 15 cm

Inscribed Welch Porcelain / Asser in gilt script on the underside of each

Purchased, 1995

NMW A 32623

This cup and saucer set is an expensive, personalised object, initialled 'JW' on the front in shaded monochrome. It was decorated, like much Nantgarw porcelain, outside of the factory. The mall blue ground and the elaborate gilding pattern are copied from fashionable Paris porcelain, and the form is inspired by that of the *tasse Jasmin* designed for the French royal factory at Sèvres. It is marked on the underside in gilt script Welch Porcelain / Asser, indicating it was sold by the firm of Henry Asser and Co, one of the principal London china dealers.

Asser's shop was at 406 Strand from 1808 to 1822, when the firm moved to the recently completed Burlington Arcade off Piccadilly, where it specialised in the sale of 'jewellery and fancy articles of fashionable demand, for the gratification of the public.'

Cabinet Cup and Saucer, 1818-1820

Decorated outside the factory, possibly in Worcester

Frit porcelain

Cup: height 8 cm.
Saucer: diameter 16.5 cm

Unmarked

Purchased, 1988

NMW A 30125

This fashionable tub-shape on lion's paw feet, often called a 'French cabinet cup,' was made by many early-nineteenth-century porcelain factories, including Spode and Swansea, so it is no surprise to find it at Nantgarw. Nantgarw examples were sold 'in the white' in London and also to the Worcester firm of Chamberlain's, where this one may have been decorated. Intriguingly, the arms are those of John Bridge (1755-1834) of Dorset, or of his nephew John Gawler Bridge (1787?-1849), partners in the great Regency firm of retail goldsmiths, Rundell, Bridge and Rundell, which also sold some porcelains.

John Jackson, *Portrait of John Bridge (1755-1834), with Piddletrenthide Church in the background*, oil on canvas, private collection © Philip Mould Ltd, London/Bridgeman Images.

Plate, 1818-1820

Decorated outside the factory, probably in London

Frit porcelain

Diameter 24.7 cm

Mark: NANT-GARW C.W impressed

Purchased, 1885

NMW A 31343

The decorator of this plate was probably an enameller called Plant. The same composition also occurs on a plate in a Derby service made for Lord Ongley in 1825; John Haslem, historian of the Derby porcelain factory, wrote of this service in 1876, 'Several were copied from Nantgarw plates, which had been decorated in London at Sim's establishment… The figure subjects on the Nantgarw plates were painted by a clever artist called Plant, and were probably the best things ever done on that china…'

Other Derby plates in the Ongley service are painted with harbour scenes within stipple gilt borders reserved with flowers, fruit, birds and butterflies and a distinctive gilding pattern inside the rim. Four more of the Nantgarw source plates acquired from Sim's by the Derby proprietor Robert Bloor are now in the Victoria and Albert Museum.

'Sim's establishment' was clearly responsible for the decoration of a significant quantity of Swansea and Nantgarw porcelain. It is said to have been in Five Fields Row, Pimlico. Spencer Simms and William Sims were both rate payers in that street from 1812 to 1826. However, a J. Sims is recorded as the proprietor of a wholesale glass warehouse in Gray's Inn Road in 1819, and a Thomas Sims as a china gilder and painter at 14 Marsham Street, Westminster in 1822. Plant may be the Chamberlain's Worcester painter James Plant or the W. Plant, enameller, who was awarded a medal by the Society of Arts in 1818, and who exhibited at the Royal Academy and the Old Water Colour Society between 1819 and 1828.

Plate, 1818-1820
Decorated outside the factory, probably in London
Frit porcelain
Diameter 25.1 cm
Mark: NANT-GARW C.W impressed
Bequeathed by David Lewis, 1994
NMW A 32352

This plate has the clear white translucency and lustrous glaze that made Nantgarw porcelain so attractive to the best china enamellers of the day. The rim moulding of C-scrolls, ribbon-tied foliage wreaths and florets is derived from Vincennes-Sèvres porcelain of the 1750s and is an early example of the nineteenth century's enthusiasm for the rococo style. It is for display rather than use. The centre is painted in enamels with a kneeling naked cupid, sitting in a lady's straw bonnet, one finger gesturing for silence.

A similar plate is known, painted with a cupid in a cage, and the message implied by the pair is probably that love unconfined can rule a woman's mind. It may have been inspired by the poetry of the Greek lyric poet Anacreon, popular during the early nineteenth century, which touched on universal themes of love, infatuation and disappointment. The design source remains untraced, and the composition may have been copied from Paris porcelain.

Plate, 1818-1820

Decorated outside the factory, probably in London

Frit porcelain

Diameter 24.9 cm

Mark: NANT GARW C.W impressed

Purchased, 1992 (Sir Leslie Joseph Collection)

NMW A 31112

The centre of the plate is painted with four doves perched on the edge of a bronze bowl. Three sun themselves, while the fourth drinks from the water it contains. The source is a mosaic of the 2nd century AD, discovered in 1737 during excavations at the palatial villa of the Roman Emperor Hadrian, near Tivoli. The mosaic, now in the Capitoline Museum in Rome, was a staple of European neoclassicism and reproduced in many media. It was also a favourite of the Berlin porcelain factory at much the same time. The gilding pattern and border of pink roses on this plate suggest that it was decorated in the Sims workshop.

The Mosaic of the Doves, Roman, 2nd century CE. Believed to be a copy of a lost ancient Greek mosaic. Capitoline Museum, Rome © Sovrintendenza Capitolina – Foto in Comune.

Plate, 1818-1820

Decorated in London

Frit porcelain

Diameter 22.8 cm

Mark: NANTGARW impressed. Also inscribed *I. Powell / 91 / Wimpole Street*

Given by Windham D. Clark, 1951

NMW A 31321

The border of this plate has an underglaze blue ground, a feature usually associated with the Young-Pardoe period at Nantgarw; but its lustrous and colourless glaze is that used by Billingsley and Walker, rather than the one employed later, which often has a greenish tinge. It bears the inscribed mark of the London china enameller John Powell, who moved from Marylebone to Wimpole Street in May 1817. There he described himself as the proprietor of a 'china warehouse' and as 'china enameller to their Royal and Imperial Highnesses the Princess Charlotte, Prince Leopold and Princess Sophia of Gloucester'. He remained there until 1820, and later worked as a teacher of china painting.

Powell also painted flowers, landscapes and costume figures, and his work is found on Swansea and Coalport as well as on imported French porcelains. The scene in the centre of this plate is taken from *Halt of a Hunting Party* by Philips Wouwerman (1619-1668), given to the Dulwich College Picture Gallery by Sir Peter Francis Bourgeois in 1811. Powell adapted the scene from a rectangular to a circular format, but he may have worked from the original painting rather than from an engraving, as he followed its colours quite closely, and the composition is not reversed.

Philips Wouwerman (1619-1668), *Halt of a Hunting Party*, oil on canvas. © Dulwich Picture Gallery.

Ice-cream pail, 1818-20

Decorated outside the factory, probably in London

Frit porcelain

Height 14.4 cm, diameter 19.8 cm

Unmarked

Given by A. R. and Miss M. Llewellin-Taylour, 1947

NMW A 31336

The Nantgarw China Works had great difficulty in firing this thickly potted upright form, copied from a model used at Sèvres from 1758, and London-decorated dessert services otherwise of Nantgarw porcelain sometimes contain ice-cream pails made by other factories. This example lacks its cover, which had a deep rim that could be packed with ice, and a high loop handle (see example, right). The ice-cream sat in the inner liner, kept cold by crushed ice.

This pail is one of two from the so-called Mackintosh dessert service of Nantgarw porcelain, and is said to have belonged to Edward Priest Richards (1791-1867), a solicitor and the Cardiff agent to the Marquess of Bute, and to have passed to his descendant Ella Mackintosh in 1880. All elements of the service are painted with brightly coloured birds. These appear to have been adapted from a number of sources including George Edwards's *Natural History of Uncommon Birds*, George Shaw's *General Zoology* and the sumptuously illustrated works of the French ornithologist François Levaillant (1753-1824).

Another Nantgarw dessert service, at least one London-decorated Paris porcelain dessert service, and a tea service were also painted in this manner. All these may have been ordered by the china dealer John Mortlock from the decorators Robbins and Randall of Barnsbury Street, Islington, and painted by Thomas Martin Randall (1786-1859).

Nantgarw ice-cream pail cover, about 1818-20.

Cream tureen, 1818-1820

Decorated in London

Frit porcelain

Mark: NANT-GARW C.W impressed (on the stand)

Height 13.4 cm, diameter 18.8 cm

Bequeathed by Ernest Morton Nance, 1952

NMW A 31326

This is one of five known cream tureen models made at Nantgarw and is notable for the crispness of the slip-cast mouldings, derived from mid-eighteenth-century French porcelain. The enamelled and gilded decoration was added in London. From the flower, bird and fruit motifs in the borders, this can be attributed to the Pall Mall workshop of John and James Bradley (see the Swansea dessert dish on p. 62).

By the late nineteenth century, it had become almost a symbol of Welsh middle-class identity to have a small collection of Swansea and Nantgarw porcelain in the home. This service, or another of the same type, then belonged to the Welsh politician and trade unionist William Brace (1865-1947).

Pieces from a dessert service, 1818-1820

Decorated outside the factory, probably in London

Frit porcelain

Pail: height 12.9

Tureen and stand: height 15.3 cm, length 36.2 cm

Centre dish: length 24.2 cm

Square dish: diameter 21.6 cm

Plates: length 21.7 cm

Mark: NANTGARW impressed (on some pieces)

Given anonymously, 1990

NMW A 30177-30212

In the early nineteenth century a dessert service usually comprised twenty-four plates, a dozen dishes (in sets of four), two pails and two small tureens for cream or sugar. All thirty-six pieces in this almost complete service have powdered green borders painted with small panels of flowers, and are richly decorated in the centre with complex bouquets of flowers and fruit. These include grapes and pomegranates, currants, and yellow carnations as well as the pink roses much used by outside decorators of Welsh porcelain. As all the compositions are different, the painter was probably following a suite of watercolour designs. The pails in this service may have been intended as bottle coolers, rather than (as was usual) containers for ice-cream, as they are lavishly decorated on the inside and lack covers and liners.

This decoration was inspired by mid-eighteenth-century porcelains from the French royal factory at Sèvres, which were already admired and collected in Regency Britain (see the Sèvres bottle cooler, right). Rather than tooling and burnishing the gilding in the time-consuming French manner, the British decorator has outlined the border cartouches in yellow enamel before applying a layer of matt gold, a technique also used at the Spode and Daniel factories in the early 1820s.

Seau (bottle cooler), soft-paste porcelain, Sèvres, 1771, decorated by Charles-Nicolas Buteux.

Plate, 1818-1820

Decorated outside the factory, probably in London

Frit porcelain

Diameter 24.4 cm

Mark: NANT-GARW C.W impressed

Purchased, 1985

NMW A 31381

Like much outside-decorated Nantgarw porcelain, this plate is painted with a design that closely copies a pattern developed at the Sèvres factory in the mid-1760s. Reflecting the simplicity and symmetry of early neo-classical ornament, this design of a turquoise ribbon entwined with a garland of flowers proved particularly popular in England. The 3rd Duke of Dorset bought a Sèvres dessert service painted with this decoration in 1770, and others were supplied to Sir Watkin Williams-Wynn and to the Earls of Carlisle and Egremont. A plate from one of these may have been used as a pattern here, and the design was later made by a number of other British factories.

Sèvres porcelain plate from a service of 1770, bought by the Duke of Dorset, Knole © National Trust / Charles Thomas.

Plate, 1818-1820
Decorated outside the factory, probably in London
Frit porcelain
Diameter 25 cm
Mark: NANT-GARW C.W impressed.
Purchased, 1992 (Sir Leslie Joseph Collection)
NMW A 31111

The Regency period saw a growing interest in the collecting and display of older European porcelains, which inspired contemporary makers to produce wares in a rococo revival manner. This unusual plate is one of a small number of Nantgarw cabinet pieces painted in imitation of Meissen porcelain of the 1730s with a Mediterranean harbour scene within a baroque strapwork cartouche. There are also smaller harbour scenes on the rim, but these are anachronistically placed within ribbon-tied C-scroll mouldings derived from a rococo model made at the Sèvres factory.

Meissen porcelain saucer with harbour scene, 1730s.

Two milk jugs, 1818-1823

Painted by Thomas Pardoe

Frit porcelain

Left: height 10.8 cm, length 16 cm
Right: height 11.1 cm, length 15.7 cm

Unmarked

Purchased, 1991 and 2012

NMW A 30229 and 39419

The jugs belong to a small group of teawares painted by Thomas Pardoe with charming vignettes of contemporary life. Similar figure compositions are recorded in the artist's sketchbooks. Both jugs show fashionably dressed children buying flowers and fruit from roadside vendors. The jug on the right includes a British soldier in a uniform datable to 1816-1822. The jugs are not a pair, but both have the reflective and almost colourless glaze used by Billingsley and Walker, rather than the creamier substitute developed by Pardoe and Young for the remaining stock of biscuit wares. The jugs may therefore have been painted soon after Pardoe's arrival in February 1821.

Watercolour from one of Thomas Pardoe's sketchbooks.

Dish, 1818-1823
Painted by Thomas Pardoe
Frit porcelain
Length 30.1 cm
Mark: NANT-GARW C. W. impressed
Purchased, 1893
NMW A 31421

This dish is painted with a view of the great 140-foot single-span bridge over the River Taff at Pontypridd, completed by William Edwards (1719-1789), Independent minister and self-taught architect. Edwards made three unsuccessful attempts before he succeeded in completing his contract in 1756. The three cylindrical holes on either side lessen the pressure on the haunches of the arch. Sometimes called 'The Bridge of Beauty', it was painted by Richard Wilson (1714-1782) and by many later artists. However, as the site is only about five miles north of Nantgarw this view is probably based on direct observation.

Exhibited in Cardiff's Fine Art and Industrial Exhibition in 1870, the dish is said to have belonged to the poet Thomas Williams (Gwilym Morgannwg (1778-1835)), who was also the publican of the New Inn, shown on the right of the engraving right.

Ponty-pryd, Glamorganshire, engraving by John Charles Varrall after a drawing by John Hassell, 1818.

Punch-bowl, 1818-1823
Painted by Thomas Pardoe
Frit porcelain
Height 12.4 cm, diameter 29.1 cm
Unmarked. Inscribed *Pen-y-Rhos*
Purchased, 1991
NMW A 30228

The farmhouse depicted is Pen-y-Rhos in the parish of Eglwysilan, with Mynydd Meio beyond. This was the home of Edward Edmunds (about 1762-1847), a successful farmer and businessman who sub-let the nearby site of the Nantgarw factory to William Billingsley and William Weston Young. He was a supportive landlord, who acted as one of Young's trustees when he went bankrupt in August 1822, and the richly gilded bowl may have been decorated as a 'thank you' around that time.

The back of the bowl shows a farmyard scene, with cattle and poultry in the foreground. The Nantgarw porcelain body was difficult to work, and the bowl is hand-thrown, and heavily potted. The glaze appears to be that used by Young from the spring of 1821.

Plate, 1818-1823
Painted by Thomas Pardoe
Frit porcelain
Diameter 21.5 cm
Mark: NANT-GARW C.W impressed
Given by W.S. de Winton, 1918
NMW A 30468

This plate was elaborately decorated by Pardoe as a 'cabinet' or ornamental piece, though one probably intended for local sale. The central vignette of two pheasants perched on a spreading branch against a moorland landscape was copied from a watercolour design in one of Pardoe's sketchbooks, which appears to be his own composition. In contrast, the shaped reserves in the underglaze blue-ground rim are painted with Pardoe's more usual and generic exotic birds. He was also a highly competent gilder, achieving here a marbled (caillouté) effect in gold against the blue, derived ultimately from Sèvres porcelain of the 1760s, which was subsequently copied at Meissen and Worcester.

A watercolour from one of Thomas Pardoe's sketchbooks.

Plate, 1818-1823
Painted at the factory
Frit porcelain
Diameter 23.8 cm
Mark: NANT-GARW C.W impressed
Bequeathed by Ernest Morton Nance, 1952
NMW A 31470

This plate belongs to a class of locally decorated Nantgarw wares loosely painted with simple subjects, mostly of oriental inspiration, in a limited enamel palette. These are sometimes called 'apprentice plates' and are said to be the work of semi-skilled painters following designs by Thomas Pardoe or one of his children. Though clearly rapidly painted, their fluid spontaneity suggests that they may in fact be by Thomas Pardoe himself, who may have developed this simple, almost naïve style to decorate service wares rapidly for sale.

The design of a chinoiserie carp in a lake-side setting was a popular one at Nantgarw, but this plate is unusual in that it has gilt detailing to the central scene, as well as the chocolate banding to the outer rim, used as a cheap alternative to gilding.

Plate, 1818-1822
Painted by Thomas Pardoe
Frit porcelain
Diameter 21.9 cm
Mark: NANT-GARW C.W impressed
Purchased, 1913
NMW A 31450

Although he was a fine painter of landscapes and figures, Thomas Pardoe was first and foremost a flower painter. He painted the centre of this plate with a pink rose, a forget-me-not and a spray of flowers and foliage. The plate has a rare pink ground rim where the relief mouldings have been left in the white. These flank vignettes of acorn sprigs and purple ranunculi.

The plate forms part of a now-dispersed dessert service made by Pardoe and Young in 1822 for Wyndham Lewis (1780-1838) of Tongwynlais, near Cardiff. Lewis, 'a thin, narrow, pale man', was lampooned by contemporaries as 'Timothy Weasel'. The fourth son of a Welsh clergymen, he began his working life in 1798 as a solicitor's clerk. By 1808 he had progressed to running his own country practice at Pentyrch, near Cardiff. The death of a childless uncle two years later transformed his life, making him and his brother major shareholders in the Dowlais Ironworks.

He was a working partner at Dowlais, credited with 'acute business acumen', and primarily concerned with accounts and managing the company's leases, contracts, property, transport and banking. He was Independent MP for the Glamorgan Boroughs 1820-1826, and subsequently sat as a Tory for English constituencies. In 1815, he married Mary Anne Evans (1792-1872), whose second husband was Benjamin Disraeli.

Wyndham Lewis (1780-1838) by Samuel William Reynolds, printed by Lahee & Co, mezzotint, early 1830s
© National Portrait Gallery, London.

The Nantgarw China Works 1813-1814 and 1816-1823

Plate, 1818-1823
Painted by Thomas Pardoe
Frit porcelain
Diameter 21.3 cm
Mark: Nantgarw in gilt script
Given by I. Louie, 1891
NMW A 31449

Plate, 1818-1823
Painted by Thomas Pardoe
Frit porcelain
Diameter 21.8 cm
Mark: NANTGARW C. W. impressed
Purchased, 1895
NMW A 30463

The plate on the left was clearly a special piece that Pardoe painted to showcase his skill. The central reserve and those on the rim were first outlined in underglaze blue, and then painted in enamels, combining two motifs often used by Pardoe on Nantgarw – an oriental man riding an elephant among palm trees, and groups of exotic birds in landscapes. The rim is marbled in pale blues and flecks of gilding, and further ornamented with Japanese flower heads in red. Very unusually, the plate is also inscribed *Nantgarw* on the back in Pardoe's distinctive script.

The plate on the right is unfinished, presumably because Pardoe died on 23 July 1823 before he could complete it. The biscuit porcelain was given a rich blue rim before it was glazed and fired. Pardoe then painted the background landscape and sketched the outlines of the rural character figures, using greens, browns and blues first as these colours required a further high temperature firing. He would have planned to fill in the figures using more delicate enamels such as red and flesh colour, before the plate was fired again at a lower temperature and gilded.

6 | The Later Cambrian Pottery 1824-1870

Lewis Weston Dillwyn regained control of the Cambrian Pottery in 1824. He travelled to Staffordshire to interview for the position of Agent to the Pottery, appointing John Hancock in March 1824. He appointed David Evans as Commercial Manager, Isaac Wood (former porcelain modeller) as Works Manager and Mr Voss became Head of the Counting-House and Chief Cashier. David Edwards replaced Hancock as Agent in 1827 and was, in turn, succeeded by James Hinckley from Stoke-on-Trent. Later census returns tell us that a proportion of the workforce, including potters, engravers and decorators, had come to work at the Cambrian Pottery from Staffordshire.[22]

Under Dillwyn's guidance, the quality of the earthenware body was considerably improved, new shapes introduced and a focus placed on transfer-printed decoration. The products were very broad-ranging, comprising mostly domestic objects but also some wares made for trades. An 1843 price list includes over a hundred different classes of object, ranging from everyday tea and dinner wares to more unusual objects such as oyster tubs, paint pallets, flower horns, myrtle pots, spitting mugs and melon moulds.[23] Tours of the Pottery could be taken, and a number of dignitaries visited, including Lord Ilchester, Lady Charlotte Talbot and Sir Humphry Davy.[24]

The Pottery principally served the local market. An advert placed in *The Cambrian* on 2 November 1827, for example, records the arrival of a ship into Cardiff with a cargo of earthenware from Swansea. Overseas trade also remained an interest for the company, including to Chile, Ireland and the Continent: *Almost every variety of earthenwares are manufactured in the "Cambrian Pottery." The produce in printed, painted, dipt, and cream-coloured wares, is chiefly disposed of at home, but the foreign trade is extending.* (*The Morning Chronicle*, Wednesday, 14 August 1850)

This new phase of the Cambrian Pottery appears to have had robust beginnings. In 1827 the business made a profit of over £1,363, despite 'many heavy debts' being incurred, not least a 'heavy & utterly unaccountable deficiency in the Pottery Stock', resulting from theft committed by George Green, Head Gloss Fireman.[25]

---

[22] Arleen Tanner, Grahame Tanner (ed.), *Swansea's Cambrian Pottery Transferware: and Other Welsh Examples* (2005), pp. 19-29

[23] Jago family papers, Cornwall Record Office, AD/194/2 (Conroy, 2018, pp. 122-124)

[24] Letter from Davy to J. H. Vivian, 20 December 1825 (National Library of Wales, Vivian Papers, ISYSARCHB67, A202)

[25] Diary of Lewis Weston Dillwyn, 29 December 1826 and 16 January 1827

In 1831 Dillwyn's second surviving son, Lewis Llewelyn, was placed in nominal charge of the Pottery. He assumed full control in 1836, though his father continued to take an interest in its affairs, overseeing, for example, the purchase and closure of the Glamorgan Pottery in 1838. It was under Lewis Llewelyn that arguably the most innovative product of the later Cambrian Pottery, 'Dillwyn's Etruscan Ware', was realised. Made between 1848 and 1850, this was a fashionable and affordable range of decorative ceramics influenced by archaeological discoveries, modelled by William Clowes and decorated using designs engraved by John Stanway Brown. While it attracted admiration from critics, it was a short-lived experiment that was not profitable.

The fortunes of the business were certainly in decline by the time Dillwyn leased the pottery to employees David Evans and John Glasson in 1850. This same year, *The Morning Chronicle* reported that the south Wales pottery trade had 'been for a considerable time in a depressed state'. The Pottery was said to employ 200 people, over half of whom were women and children, including some as young as eight years old.[26]

The article in *The Morning Chronicle* notes that the Pottery was consuming 3,300 tons of coal each year, a 17.5% reduction from 4,000 tons at full capacity. The working day was twelve hours long, beginning at 6am. These extremely long days meant that the children would have received very limited schooling.[27] Wages were paid on a piece-work basis, and income for male workers had fallen by up to a third. Many of the women and children were employed by the men, so their earnings would have reduced at a similar rate.

The death of Glasson at his Plymouth home in March 1852, aged 47, would have been a further blow. Over the course of the next eighteen years, the quality of the products diminished in parallel with the failing fortunes of the business. The lease was relinquished by Evans in 1870, and production at the Cambrian Pottery ceased.

---

[26] The 1842 factory inspection lists 238 employees, including 48 between 13 and 18 years of age and 22 under 13 years of age (Ian Winstanley (ed.), Children's Employment Commission 1842. South Wales 2, Wigan, 1999, p. 14). Census returns for 1851 suggest the workforce was probably smaller by that date

[27] Grant-Davidson, 2010, Appendix IV

Punch bowl, 1845
Designed by George Grant Francis, FSA
Painted by Stephen Dingley
Enamelled and gilded earthenware
Diameter 36.8 cm
Mark: Made at Dillwyn / Pottery Swansea (hand-painted in black enamel)
Purchased, 1996
NMW A 32643

This impressive punch bowl was presented to John Crow Richardson (1842-1903) of Swansea by his grandfather, John Richardson (1790-1858). It is a companion and near pair to a bowl that was presented to John Richardson Francis, and is now in the Glynn Vivian Art Gallery's collection. John Richardson gave the bowls to his infant grandsons to mark their birthdays, in the year he was Mayor of Swansea.

Born in South Shields, John Richardson came to Swansea in 1826 and became one of the town's principal shipbuilders, constructing vessels for the copper trade. His business interests were varied and included a partnership in the Liverpool Packet Steam Company, which operated the first paddle-steamer service between Swansea and Liverpool. John Crow Richardson followed his father to become Director of the Glamorganshire Banking Company and also invested in coal mining. He became High Sherriff of Carmarthenshire in 1893.[28]

George Grant Francis (1814-1882) was married to John Richardson's daughter, Sarah, and designed a bowl each for their son and (this one) for their nephew. He was a prominent Swansea antiquarian, helping to found the Cambrian Archaeological Association and Royal Institution of South Wales. He represented the Swansea district as local commissioner for the Great Exhibition of 1851[29].

---

[28] M. Richardson and P. Richardson, *The Richardsons of Swansea. Ship Owners and Copper Merchants*, (2010), privately published

[29] G. Goodwin, revised by B. Jones, 'Francis, George Grant (1814-1882)', *Oxford Dictionary of National Biography* (accessed 20/08/21)

Jug, about 1850

Transfer-printed pearlware

Height 35 cm

Unmarked

Purchased, 1992 (Sir Leslie Joseph Collection)

NMW A 31125

This large jug might have been produced for display in a warehouse or shop, to showcase the quality and diversity of Cambrian Pottery printed wares, as it uses four printing colours and filled-in decoration. The large print of the 'Oriental Basket' pattern at the centre of the composition was introduced around 1836. It is surrounded by a broad variety of smaller vignettes including pastoral and patriotic naval scenes, Masonic imagery and 'Courtship and Matrimony'. Many of these prints are not otherwise recorded on Cambrian Pottery.

The jug incorporates a rich and complex array of emblematic messages and an alternative possibility is that it was commissioned by or for a client with links to Cornwall. The decorative scheme includes several repeats of fifteen bezants in pile – a motif of dots arranged to form an inverted triangle – which is a heraldic device for Cornwall. Another unusual feature is the inclusion of Welsh inscriptions, *ALLWEDD CALON CWRW DA / CYMRI DROS BYTH* ('The key to the heart is good beer / Wales forever') and *CYMRY FU, CYMRY FYDD* ('Once Wales, Always Wales' or 'Once a Welshman, Always a Welshman'), as well as the anglicised Irish phrase *ERIN GO BRAGH* ('Ireland Forever'). Such inscriptions are rarely found on Cambrian wares, which supports an argument that it was a special commission.

Plates, about 1825-1830
Earthenware
Diameter 20 cm
Mark: DILLWYN & Co. SWANSEA (impressed)
Given by Mrs C. Scoble, 1932
Bequeathed by Ernest Morton Nance, 1952
NMW A 31536 & 31537

Wicker-border plates were decorative objects, for display rather than use. A coloured ribbon could be threaded through the pierced edge, as seen on the plate on the right. Similar designs were made at the Glamorgan Pottery and the Moore Pottery in Sunderland.

Named after the shimmering colours used for its decoration, lustreware began to be produced commercially in Britain during the early nineteenth century. The pink lustre used to decorate these plates was made from a powdered compound of gold and tin.

Despite its broader popularity, lustreware was made in small quantities during the later phase of the Cambrian Pottery and tended to be used for decorating jugs and wicker-border plates. An 1843 price list tells us that lustre was the most expensive type of standard decoration available at that time. A dozen six-inch plates with lustre cost 2s 3d, examples with 'Best Blue, Blk. & Green' printing were 2s, those with 'Willow' cost 1s 2d and undecorated plate cost just 8d a dozen.[30]

[30] See note 24

The Later Cambrian Pottery 1824-1870

Cow Creamer, about 1830-1838
Glamorgan Pottery, Swansea
Transfer-printed earthenware
Length 17.4 cm
Mark: Opaque / China / BB&I (printed in a ribbon and cartouche)
Bequeathed by Ernest Morton Nance, 1952
NMW A 31891

Cow Creamer, about 1825-1835
Transfer-printed earthenware
Length 17.8 cm
Unmarked
Bequeathed by Ernest Morton Nance, 1952
NMW A 31587

Cow creamers – novelty items used to serve milk or cream at tea – were made by many British manufacturers during the nineteenth century. The cream is poured into the jug through an opening on the back, and the handle is formed by the tail. The design was probably inspired by examples in silver, made in England during the second half of the eighteenth century by makers such as John Schuppe.

Cow creamers were made at both the Cambrian and Glamorgan Potteries and were most often decorated with transfer prints. The Cambrian jug has a design of shells and scrolls to one side and a floral sprig to the reverse, while the Glamorgan example has two complementary fishing scenes that were used on a variety of domestic objects. Although the creamers are very similar in form and size, they were not made from the same mould; the Cambrian Pottery creamers are traditionally described as having a more prominent breastbone than their Glamorgan counterparts.

Teapot, about 1825-1835
Transfer-printed earthenware
Length 27.3 cm
Unmarked
Bequeathed by Ernest Morton Nance, 1952
NMW A 31559

Teapot, about 1827-1835
Transfer-printed earthenware
Length 27 cm
Mark: small cross (moulded)
Bequeathed by Ernest Morton Nance, 1952
NMW A 31524

Sugar box, about 1825-1835
Transfer-printed earthenware
Length 17.9 cm
Mark: Mignionette (printed)
Bequeathed by Ernest Morton Nance, 1952
NMW A 31521

The elongated oblong form of these teawares is commonly known as the 'London' shape. The design is probably taken from contemporary examples in silver or silver plate. Each object is transfer-printed with a fashionable pattern and illustrates three of the different colours for printing used at the Cambrian Pottery during the 1820s and 1830s.

Polite pastimes were popular subjects for transfer decoration in the early nineteenth century and 'Lady Archers' (centre) was introduced during the 1820s. Variants of the pattern are found on teawares, jugs and coffee pots. Similar patterns are known from several different factories, including Wedgwood. 'Swan and Flying Bird' is a similar but more stylised design. It features a swan on a lake with a flying bird to the left side, with pagoda buildings in the background. The scene is bordered with an asymmetric design incorporating sprays of flowers, foliage and scrolls, and to the left side, a water fountain. On both teapots joins are clearly visible where the paper transfer was trimmed to fit.

The sugar box is decorated with a pattern called 'Mignionette', which is the earliest sheet pattern used at the Cambrian Pottery. A sheet pattern is composed of repeated motifs with no distinct centre or edge, meaning it can be printed across the entire surface of an object.

Group of 'Etruscan Wares', 1847-1850

Transfer-printed earthenware

Maximum height 25.8 cm

Mark: DILLWYN'S / ETRUSCAN / WARE (printed)

Bequeathed by Ernest Morton Nance, 1952; purchased, 1906 (two-handled dish/kylix)

NMW A 31820, 31827, 31832, 31835 & 31847

Made under the close supervision of Lewis Llewelyn Dillwyn, 'Dillwyn's Etruscan Ware' was arguably the most innovative and distinctive product of the late Cambrian Pottery. Made using iron-rich clay from the Dillwyn family estate of Penllergaer, this fashionable and affordable range of art pottery was inspired by contemporary archaeological discoveries that had stimulated an interest in the classical world.

The Cambrian Pottery was not alone in responding to this desire for classically inspired design, and similar lines were produced in ceramics and glass by companies such as Wedgwood and Richardson's of Stourbridge. The shapes were modelled by William Clowes and decorated using designs engraved by John Stanway Brown. It has been argued that Dillwyn's wife, Bessie, contributed to the development of Etruscan Ware, though recent research has questioned this assumption. The Etruscan Ware was not a commercial success, and production ceased when the business was transferred to David Evans and John Glasson.

Vase, about 1825

Transfer-printed earthenware

Height 43.6 cm

Mark: SWANSEA over crossed tridents (impressed)

Purchased, 1954

NMW A 31771

This ornamental vase might have functioned as a pastille burner. They are usually smaller in size, but this example might have been influenced by Wedgwood's introduction of large pastille burners in the early nineteenth century. Pastilles were small, cone-shaped objects made from charcoal powder impregnated with fragrant oils. When lit in a burner, they released a pleasant scent into the room.

This vase (missing its cover) and its companion pair are the only recorded examples of this shape. The vase has the impressed 'trident' mark used on the porcelain body of the same name developed during the later period of the Swansea China Works, which is otherwise unknown on earthenware objects.

Bottle, 1850
Evans & Glasson
Transfer-printed earthenware
Height 16.5 cm
Unmarked
Given by W. J. Grant-Davidson, 1994
NMW A 32254

Bulbous bottles of this type were probably intended for ale or cider and would originally have had a cork stopper. The handle form is seen on large mugs but the body is wheel-thrown and perhaps unique. The monogram 'R M / 1850' suggests it was a special commission. The sheet pattern of fruiting currants, printed in blue, is not recorded on any other Cambrian object.

Each side of the jug is printed with a monochrome scene in reserve. The dramatic view of a bustling 'SWANSEA HARBOUR AND TOWN' is after a print published by J. Newman of Watling Street, London. The second commemorates Queen Victoria's visit to Place House in Fowey, Cornwall, on 8 September 1846. Joseph Thomas Treffry (1782-1850) was the owner of Place House at the time of the visit. Treffry was an enterprising man with wide-ranging business interests, including a china clay works in the St Dennis area of Cornwall that supplied numerous potteries in Staffordshire.

Jug, about 1860-1870

D. J. Evans & Co

Transfer-printed and enamelled earthenware

Height 22.6 cm

Mark: D. J. EVANS & CO/ BIRDS/ SWANSEA (printed)

Given by F. Emile Andrews, 1932

NMW A 31742

This jug was made during the Cambrian Pottery's final years, while it was under the leadership of David Evans, following John Glasson's death. The transfer-printed wares made during this period lack the ambition and finesse of earlier production, and appear to reflect the declining fortunes of the business.

The jug is printed with two images from the 'Birds' series – one of the few new pattern ranges introduced during this later phase. On one side is a scene of two birds perched on branches in a woodland setting, and on the reverse, a group of small game birds in a forest clearing, with a fox emerging from shrubbery. 'Birds' patterns appear to be restricted to this particular type of jug and are usually printed in underglaze blue or brown with overpainted enamels. The simple, pear-shaped jug form was also produced at the Llanelly Pottery.

Plate, about 1840
Dillwyn & Co.
Transfer-printed earthenware
Diameter: 15.8 cm
Unmarked
Bequeathed by Ernest Morton Nance, 1952
NMW A 31638

Plate, 1838
Dillwyn & Co.
Transfer-printed earthenware
Diameter 15.9 cm
Mark: DILLWYN / SWANSEA (impressed)
Bequeathed by Ernest Morton Nance, 1952
NMW A 31627

Plate, about 1840
Dillwyn & Co.
Transfer-printed and enamelled earthenware
Diameter 21.3 cm
Mark: DILLWYN & CO / 1 (impressed)
Bequeathed by Ernest Morton Nance, 1952
NMW A 31621

St Michael's Mount is a tidal island in Mount's Bay, west Cornwall. At low tide it can be reached on foot via a causeway from the harbour in the town of Marazion. The church and castle seen at the island's summit were built in the medieval period and today are managed by the National Trust.

A number of commemorative wares were made by the Cambrian Pottery about 1840. Queen Victoria's coronation was the subject of one such object, which was produced alongside a portrait plate of Prince Albert. The plate depicting the temperance reformer James Tear Preston is one of a series that also included the Methodist founder John Wesley and theologian John William Fletcher.

Jug, 1825-1830

Dillwyn & Co.

Transfer-printed earthenware

Diameter 25.8 cm

Mark: DILLWYN & CO SWANSEA (impressed)

Bequeathed by Ernest Morton Nance, 1952

NMW A 31763

Plate, 1825-1830

Dillwyn & Co.

Transfer-printed earthenware

Height 25.2 cm

Bequeathed by Ernest Morton Nance, 1952

NMW A 31762

These objects are both printed with the 'Women with Baskets' pattern, which is probably unique to the Cambrian Pottery. It depicts two women and a young man by a stream. The women are laden with baskets and are possibly washing clothes. The pattern was printed in various colours including black, blue and puce.

Jugs, 1835-1850

Dillwyn & Co.

Enamelled, lustred and sprigged earthenware

Maximum height 19 cm

Mark: CYMRO/STONE/CHINA (moulded; NMW A 31599-600, NMW A 31678)

Mark: [cartouche] (impressed, NMW A 31604)

Bequeathed by Ernest Morton Nance, 1952; given by Miss Florence S. Nicholas, 1933; given by Mrs E. Knibbs, 1939

NMW A 31608-9, 31599-600, 31604, 31678

This group of pouch-shaped jugs illustrates the diversity of hand-decorating techniques employed by the Cambrian Pottery from about 1835 to 1850, including enamelling, lustre, sprigging and the use of coloured glazes and slips. Two also have personal inscriptions. The first was presented to Reverend William Howells in 1847, who became Principal of Trefeca Calvinistic College, near Talgarth. The second is dedicated to Reverend Howells's wife, Margaret Morgan of Glanbrydain, and given to her the same year by Mary Ann Morris, to whom Morton Nance attributed the decoration.

Two of the jugs are 'sprigged' with flowers and fruiting vines, which have been moulded and applied to the surface. The 1842 report into the employment of children in south Wales records the experience of Thomas James, aged 14, who had worked at the Cambrian Pottery for four years. He describes his work as making 'figures in moulds for putting on the sides of the ware.' He worked twelve-hour days and was paid 3s 6d a week by his master. He was one of 70 children under 18 years of age employed in the factory at the time of its inspection.

7 | The Glamorgan Pottery 1813-1838

In 1810 George Haynes left the Cambrian Pottery following twenty-one years of service, his relationship with Lewis Weston Dillwyn irrevocably damaged by an acrimonious and very public dispute. Following his departure – and perhaps as an irritant to Dillwyn – Haynes promptly founded the South Wales Soap Works on the site of an old foundry next to the Cambrian Pottery. The smell created by the production of this soap was so noxious that it drove away visitors and potential clients. It caused many workers at the Pottery to become ill and forced at least one, Thomas Green, to resign.[31] Dillwyn suspected deliberate sabotage ('Soap works began on 12th March: Stench began 13th March,' he wrote) and took legal action for the damage to his business, forcing Haynes to abandon his new venture.

The Glamorgan Pottery was conceived and financed by Haynes as a direct competitor to the Cambrian Pottery and was trading by 1813. This brand-new business was built next to its long-established rival, with equally good access to the canal. It was managed by Haynes's son-in-law, William Baker, who had worked at the Cambrian Pottery and was the only other partner with any experience in the trade. Baker held the largest share in the company, the rest divided between partners William Bevan senior, William Bevan junior, Robert Bevan, Martin Bevan and Thomas Irwin.

---

[31] National Library of Wales, Penllergaer, D61

The early years of the Glamorgan Pottery coincided with a dramatic increase in the volume of pottery shipped out of Swansea, which rose from 50,993 pieces in 1812 to 140,280 in 1819.[32] There was clearly a large and increasing demand for ceramics during this period and the likelihood is that the Pottery was doing good business. It produced a very broad range of good-quality domestic earthenware including jugs, tea sets, dinner services, toilet sets and decorative goods such as ship plates. Moulded jugs in varying sizes were perhaps the most commonly manufactured product. The Glamorgan wares were predominantly decorated with a large range of transfer-printed patterns, most often in blue but also black, green, pink, purple and brown. While there was a degree of interchange with the Cambrian Pottery, many of the Glamorgan Pottery's decorative designs and shapes were unique to the factory. Examples of hand-painted decoration are comparatively rare, but include some jugs, wicker-border plates with pierced edges and others with 'filled-in' transfer decoration.

William Baker's death in 1819 meant that the Pottery lost its senior partner and major shareholder. Managerial responsibility for the Pottery passed to the Bevan family though Baker's wife, Hannah, maintained shares in the company. A second serious blow was the failure in 1829 of the Bevans's business, the Landore Iron Company, based in Morriston. Three members of the Bevan family were forced to declare bankruptcy, meaning their shares in the stock and buildings of the Glamorgan Pottery had to be sold to satisfy creditors, though they ultimately remained in the Bevan family.[33] The death of George Haynes in 1830 and Hannah Baker in 1835 would have been felt deeply by the remaining partners as the business continued to fail. In 1832, William Weston Young considered taking the lease for the Pottery to further his experiments in making porcelain, though this did not come to fruition.

Lewis Weston Dillwyn and Lewis Llewelyn Dillwyn met Martin Bevan in November 1837 'on the subject of a proposed purchase of the Glamorgan Pottery'.[34] The sale was agreed in July 1838 and Lewis shut the business down, permanently ridding the Cambrian Pottery of its nearest rival. Auctions of the remaining stock were advertised in *The Bristol Mercury* in May and September of the following year, aimed at 'families and dealers in ware', with further sales specifically for the trade.

---

[32] Hallesy, 1995, p. 8

[33] Hallesy (1995), pp. 9-10

[34] Lewis Weston Dillwyn diary entry, 18 November 1837

Jug, 1829
Baker, Bevans & Irwin, Glamorgan Pottery, Swansea
Painted by William Pollard
Enamelled pearlware
Height 18.5 cm
Unmarked
Purchased, 1905
NMW A 31890

Often referred to as the 'Glamorgan shape', this jug is a standard form made in large quantities at the Glamorgan Pottery and also produced at Llanelli in the 1840s. This particular example is very unusual as it has been hand-painted with sprays of wild and cultivated flowers, rather than transfer-printed, as was most common. The decoration has been attributed to William Pollard (1803-1854), who is best known for his work on Swansea porcelain where he specialised in the painting of flowers.

It was probably decorated by Pollard at his premises on King Street, Carmarthen, where he had set up business as a 'China Manufacturer, and Dealer in Glass and Earthenware'. It has the monogram 'J W / 1829' in gilt script.

The Glamorgan Pottery 1813-1838

Plate, 1813-1830

Baker, Bevans & Irwin, Glamorgan Pottery, Swansea

Transfer-printed and enamelled earthenware

Diameter 11.3 cm

Mark: BAKER BEVANS & IRWIN / SWANSEA circling Prince of Wales feathers (impressed)

Bequeathed by Ernest Morton Nance, 1952

NMW A 31873

Plate, 1813-1830

Baker, Bevans & Irwin, Glamorgan Pottery, Swansea

Transfer-printed and enamelled earthenware

Diameter 12.7 cm

Mark: BAKER BEVANS & IRWIN / SWANSEA / 4 (impressed)

Bequeathed by Ernest Morton Nance, 1952

NMW A 31867

These two small ornamental plates were probably designed for children. It is sobering therefore to consider that at the time these plates were made, the exploitation of child labour was rife within the pottery industry, including the potteries in south Wales.

The plates are transfer-printed and roughly overpainted, or 'filled in', with polychrome enamels. While very cheap to produce, they are nevertheless charming celebrations of childhood. The first plate is decorated with a basket of fruit with a bird standing atop, circled by a moulded border with flowers, foxes, cats and dogs. The second depicts 'Infancy, Youth, Manhood and Old Age', as illustrated by a multi-generational family gathering. Its border is moulded with honeysuckle and roses.

Jug, 1832

Baker, Bevans & Irwin, Glamorgan Pottery, Swansea

Transfer-printed earthenware

Height 15.7 cm

Mark: 8 (impressed)

Bequeathed by Ernest Morton Nance, 1952

NMW A 31857

Jug, 1832

Baker, Bevans & Irwin, Glamorgan Pottery, Swansea

Transfer-printed earthenware

Height 15.6 cm

Mark: Opaque / China / BB&I (transfer printed)

Bequeathed by Ernest Morton Nance, 1952

NMW A 31858

These jugs commemorate the eventual passing of the Great Reform Bill by Lord Grey's Whig government in June 1832. This followed earlier failed attempts to gain a majority vote in its favour. The Bill reallocated seats in the House of Commons and enlarged the electorate, thereby 'restoring the purity of the constitution'. It is probably the political event most commonly commemorated on British ceramics during the early nineteenth century.

The moulded jug includes portraits of Lord Brougham and Lord John Russell, both of whom were closely associated with the cause of reform. Larger jugs also include portraits of Lord Althorp and Lord Grey. Both jugs include prints of two hands clasped in agreement in a wreath garland, repeated around the neck.

Meat plate, about 1820-1838
Baker, Bevans & Irwin, Glamorgan Pottery, Swansea
Transfer-printed earthenware
Length 37.7 cm
Mark: BAKER BEVANS & IRWIN (impressed)
Bequeathed by Ernest Morton Nance, 1952
NMW A 31888

This large meat plate is transfer-printed with the 'Ladies of Llangollen' pattern, which was used at both the Cambrian and Glamorgan Potteries. It is traditionally said to represent Lady Eleanor Butler (1739-1829) and Miss Sarah Ponsonby (1755-1831) riding in the countryside. The two women met in 1768 and fell in love. Sarah and Eleanor persistently fought to be together and, following an unsuccessful attempt to elope, they left Ireland with the permission of their families.

They moved to Wales in 1778 and Plas Newydd, in the town of Llangollen, became their home. The women were extraordinarily well-known in their lifetimes and many notable individuals either visited or corresponded with them, including William Wordsworth, Percy Shelley, Richard Brinsley Sheridan, Josiah Wedgwood, Anna Seward, Anne Lister and Arthur Wellesley, later Duke of Wellington.[35] A pair of porcelain chocolate cups once owned by Sarah and Eleanor is in the collection of the British Museum.[36]

---

[35] Elizabeth Mavor, 'Butler, Lady (Charlotte) Eleanor (1739-1829)', *Oxford Dictionary of National Biography*, https://doi.org/10.1093/ref:odnb/4182 (accessed 18 December 2020)

[36] One of the cups has the gilt monogram 'SP', the other 'EB'. They are enamelled with views of Plas Newydd and the arms of the Butler and Ponsonby families (accession number 1887, 0307,VIII.34)

Ewer and basin, about 1830-1838

Baker, Bevans & Irwin, Glamorgan Pottery, Swansea

Transfer-printed earthenware

Jug: height 25.4 cm. Bowl: diameter 34.2 cm

Mark: Opaque / China / BB&I (transfer printed)

Bequeathed by Ernest Morton Nance, 1952

NMW A 31901 and 31902

This ewer and basin form a chamber set, used for washing in the bedchamber. Moulded jugs in a wide range of sizes were the most common products of the Glamorgan Pottery. The moulded pattern around the rim of the bowl and jug is called 'gadrooning' and is taken directly from comparable objects in silver and silver plate. Both objects are transfer printed with a romantic Italianate landscape called the 'Tower' pattern, with a second, complex border pattern of flowers in scrolling rococo cartouches.

The majority of goods produced at the factory in the 1820s and 1830s were transfer-printed, and over seventy different patterns are thought to have been in use.

Broth bowl, cover and stand, about 1830-1838

Baker, Bevans & Irwin, Glamorgan Pottery, Swansea

Transfer-printed earthenware

Bowl: length 19.1 cm

Mark: Opaque / China / BB&I (transfer printed)

Acquired by exchange from Shapland Dobbs, 1916

NMW A 31911

This broth bowl is very unusual as it is made in a buff-coloured earthenware, sometimes referred to as 'drab ware'. The stand is decorated with a chinoiserie garden print that includes two figures, one holding a parasol and the other a lantern, with two others standing in a stylised pagoda. The interior and cover of the bowl are printed with a figurative print, showing a woman with a small child riding a dog.

8 | The South Wales Pottery 1840-1922

The town of Llanelli in Carmarthenshire saw significant industrial growth during the mid-nineteenth century. In addition to a number of collieries, works for refining and processing copper, tin and lead were established, with products exported from the town's port. In 1840, William Chambers junior, a local businessman and magistrate, opened his newly built South Wales Pottery, or Llanelly Pottery, adding a further trade to Llanelli's flourishing economy.

The closure of the Glamorgan Pottery in 1838 meant that the new venture benefitted from the availability of a sizable group of experienced potters seeking employment. The South Wales Pottery's first manager, William Bryant, had previously worked at both the Cambrian and Glamorgan Potteries. By 1841, Chambers had built over fifty houses along two streets near the business – Pottery Row and Pottery Place – and many of his employees settled in these terraces.

By 1851, the South Wales Pottery employed over 120 people. It included potters originally from Swansea and others from Staffordshire; some probably arrived via the Glamorgan Pottery, but others are known to have come directly to Llanelli for work.[37] Typically, a proportion of the workers were women and children. The 1851 census lists, for example, Jane Thomas, aged 9, as a 'Painter in Pottery' and Joseph Henshall, aged 7, as 'Employed in the Pottery'. On 27 July 1894, the *Western Mail* reported that management had sought to improve conditions by reducing the working day for adults and children of both sexes to a maximum of eight hours, or forty-eight hours per week. However, workmen apparently claimed that 'a day of eight hours is not long enough to enable them to complete a fair day's work, and they claim that they were better off under the old regime', to which they had reverted.

Following the death of his father in 1855, Chambers leased the Pottery to Charles William Coombs and William Thomas Holland for a short period, but the partnership ran into financial difficulty. Holland renegotiated the lease and continued alone, before being joined by David Guest in 1868. Although it primarily served the local market, overseas trade became increasingly important and, prior to the First World War, goods were exported to the East Indies, North and South America and continental Europe.[38] The Pottery had a stand at the London International Exhibition of 1862, suggesting the quality of its finest wares was recognised within the trade.

---

[37] Gareth Hughes and Robert Pugh, *Llanelly Pottery* (1990), p. 31

[38] Dilys Jenkins, *Llanelly Pottery* (1968), p. 35; Llewellynn Jewitt, *The Ceramic Art of Great Britain*, London, (1878), p. 573

The South Wales Pottery principally made traditional domestic earthenware, such as toilet sets and dinner services, described as 'equal in quality to the average Staffordshire make',[39] along with some ornamental wares. Decoration was typically transfer-printed, although hand-painted and filled-in patterns were also produced. It acquired numerous copper printing plates from the Cambrian Pottery following its closure in 1870, as well as some from smaller failed businesses such as the Ynysmeudwy Pottery at Pontardawe. A number of well-known Cambrian and Glamorgan Pottery shapes were also directly reproduced. Experiments were undertaken to create coloured bodies, including different tones of blue and a buff coloured-ware, though these appear to have been made in small numbers. Perhaps most surprising is the short-lived manufacture of lithophanes, which was almost certainly the factory's only venture into porcelain production.

Further financial problems saw the Pottery closed once more in 1875 and re-opened in 1877 by Guest and Richard Dewsberry. The designs of the early twentieth century are certainly the most progressive made at the Pottery. Of particular note are the distinctive hand-painted wares, including objects with roses and fruit that can be compared stylistically to products of the Pountney Pottery in Bristol and Fife's Weymss Pottery. The 'Cockerel Plates', traditionally attributed to Sarah Jane Roberts or 'Aunt Sal' (1859-1935), have over time become synonymous with the South Wales Pottery. Despite this period of innovation, the business continued steadily to decline, and a limited company was formed by the Guest family in 1912. The last firing took place in 1922, and the Llanelly Pottery finally closed its doors.

---

[39] Jelinger Symons, *The Industrial Capacities of South Wales*, London, (1855), p. 28

Bust, about 1840-1855
Enamelled earthenware
Height 27.1 cm
Mark: W.CHAMBERS.JUNIOR/SOUTH WALES/POTTERY (impressed)
Bequeathed by Ernest Morton Nance, 1952
NMW A 32012

This is one of only two known busts of John Wesley (1703-1791) made at the South Wales Pottery; the second is in the collection at Parc Howard Museum in Llanelli. It is based on a fine example that was modelled from life by Enoch Wood in 1781. It was subsequently produced at his pottery in Burslem, Staffordshire, and widely copied by other manufacturers.

Wesley was a Church of England clergyman and the founder of Methodism, who is known to have visited Llanelli on several occasions. It is said that Methodism was first introduced to Llanelli by Wilfred Colley, butler to Sir Thomas Stepney of Llanelli House, who became an influential figure in the growth of Methodism in the town.

Lithophane, about 1850-1855
Porcelain
Height 16.5 cm
Mark: SOUTH WALES POTTERY (impressed)
Purchased, 2008
NMW A 39081

Lithophanes are ornamental plaques moulded in porcelain which, when placed in front of a light, reveal a hidden image. This example depicts a young woman reaching though a fence to pick a bunch of grapes. Very few lithophanes are believed to have been made at Llanelli, and marked pieces are extremely rare. The first examples came to light in 1921, in the possession of a former foreman of the pottery. Four of these were acquired by Amgueddfa Cymru that same year, though only two are now thought to have been made at the South Wales Pottery. In 1855, barrister Jelinger Symons described these curiosities as 'transparent tableaus of imitation Parian are beautifully executed… at a trifling cost'.[40]

---

[40] Jelinger Symons, *The Industrial Capacities of South Wales,* London, (1855), p. 28

Meat dish, about 1840-1855

Transfer-printed earthenware

Length 50.5 cm

Mark: DAMASK BORDER/SOUTH/WALES POTTERY (transfer-printed)

Bequeathed by Ernest Morton Nance, 1952

NMW A 31976

Cheese stand, about 1840-1855

Transfer-printed earthenware

Diameter 31.3 cm

Mark: DAMASK BORDER/SOUTH/WALES POTTERY (transfer-printed)

Bequeathed by Ernest Morton Nance, 1952

NMW A 31974

Sauce tureen and stand, about 1840-1855

Transfer-printed earthenware

Length 23 cm

Mark: DAMASK/BORDER/SOUTH/WALES POTTERY (transfer-printed)

Bequeathed by Ernest Morton Nance, 1952

NMW A 31975

These three objects are transfer-printed with the 'Damask Border' pattern, which is unique to the South Wales Pottery. It was used for both table and toilet wares. The border is a clever imitation of damask or watered silk, with a fashionable Italianate countryside scene at its centre. The quality of the printing on the meat dish is especially fine. The scrolling rococo border casts a shadow onto the edge of the damask, giving it a beautiful sense of depth. The range of tones captured in the print is also extremely sophisticated – from the subtle suggestion of clouds to the shimmering, variegated tones of the silk.

Vase, about 1840-1860

Transfer-printed earthenware

Height 32.1 cm

Mark: PANORAMA / SOUTH / WALES POTTERY (transfer-printed)

Bequeathed by Ernest Morton Nance, 1952

NMW A 31995

This vase is decorated with the 'Panorama' pattern, which is found printed in blue, green, brown and black. Although it is thought to be unique to the South Wales Pottery, it is typical of the many patterns produced by contemporary British potteries illustrating named or imaginary views of the countryside in Europe and further afield. The ornate shape reflects the renewed interest in rococo design during the mid-nineteenth century. The flaring neck is reminiscent of the form of the vase *à oreilles*, introduced at Sèvres in 1754, which was copied by Minton in Staffordshire from the 1840s.

Teapot, 1840-1850
Stoneware
Length 21.7 cm
Mark: SOUTH WALES/POTTERY and PRINCE ALBERT (both impressed)
Given by Shapland Dobbs, 1920
NMW A 31972

The South Wales Pottery made a few experimental coloured ceramic bodies during the mid-nineteenth century, including this bright powder-blue stoneware. The teapot combines a low round shape and fantastical bird's-head spout fashionable in the late 1830s, with an elaborately moulded body reminiscent of contemporary stoneware jugs. The 'Prince Albert' mark suggests that it might date from around the time of his marriage to Queen Victoria in 1840.

The 1841 census returns for Llanelli provide information on some of the individuals who specialised in making moulded wares at the factory. These included David Augustus (aged 16), Henry Foster (aged 27), brothers Daniel and John Davies (aged 21 and 19) and Joseph Phelps (aged 21). They are described either as 'moulder', 'potter presser' or 'potter squeezer', indicating that they made press-moulded objects. John Rees (aged 30) worked as a 'slipmaker' and would have prepared the liquid slip for making slip-cast objects.

Bowl, about 1912
Enamelled earthenware
Diameter 25.5 cm
Mark: Llanelly (hand-painted in black)
Given by Martin Phillips, 1937
NMW A 32044

Plate, about 1910
Enamelled earthenware
Diameter 24.7 cm
Mark: Llanelly (stencilled in green)
Given by Martin Phillips, 1938
NMW A 32046

These two objects are examples of the characterful hand-painted wares produced at Llanelli in the early twentieth century. Flowers and fruit are common subjects, but figurative work is much rarer. The plate is one of several examples produced at the pottery bearing the image of Mari Jones, a Welsh folk heroine. In 1800, aged fifteen, Jones is said to have walked over twenty-five miles barefoot through the mountains of Gwynedd to purchase a copy of the bible from Reverend Thomas Charles of Bala.

Upon reaching the town, one version of the story tells that the Reverend had no bibles to sell, but upon hearing Jones's plight he paid for her to stay in the town until new supplies arrived two days later. One of the bibles bought by Jones is in the National Library of Wales in Aberystwyth.

Biscuit jar, 1912
Probably painted by Samuel Shufflebotham
Sponged and enamelled earthenware
Height 16.3 cm
Mark: Llanelly / Pottery (stencilled in black)
Purchased, 1987
NMW A 32029

This biscuit jar was given as a wedding gift to 'Mr & Mrs David' on the occasion of their marriage. The recipients were probably Frederick Charles David and Janet Evans, who were married at Meidrim, Carmarthen, on 24 February 1912 (though the date on the jar is the 25th). The gift is thought to have been given to the couple by Fred's sister-in-law, whose relative worked as a packer in the factory. Samuel Shufflebotham (1876-1939) was born in Staffordshire, and also worked at the Pountney pottery in Bristol.

Cabaret tea set, about 1910
Enamelled earthenware
Tray: length 31.3 cm
Mark: LLANELLY / POTTERY (stencilled in black)
Given by Martin Phillips, 1937
NMW A 32047-32051

This cabaret service, hand painted with dog roses, is designed for making and serving tea for one person. The jug and bowl are especially rare, as they were only made as part of a cabaret set. Decoration of this particular style and quality is usually attributed to Samuel Shufflebotham, a specialist painter at Llanelli. The roses are painted in a very similar manner to examples produced at the Weymss factory in Scotland. Before working at the South Wales Pottery, Shufflebotham worked at Pountneys in Bristol. There he worked with George Stewart, who had previously worked for Weymss and must have influenced Shufflebotham.

Presented to Mr & Mrs David
on their marriage
Feby 25 1912
by Mrs R.P. David.

9 | The Leading Figures

George Haynes (1745-1830)

George Haynes[41] was born in Kingston-upon-Thames, Surrey. He went to America in 1765, and by 1780 was well established in Philadelphia. He had a large shipping and merchant business trading with Ireland, Spain and the Caribbean. In 1782 he was one of the first directors of the Bank of North America. In 1785 he left for Britain, and by 1789 had arrived in Swansea, where he entered into partnership with John Coles at the Swansea Pottery.

Haynes had intended to retire and carry on 'some little business to employ him', but found that the Swansea Pottery was, in fact, no 'nice easy employment.' He was largely – if not wholly – responsible for organizing the Pottery on 'Mr Wedgwood's plan', introducing new management principles and greater diversity and quality of output.

This, and his focus on the American market, helped the Pottery become one of the most successful of Wedgwood's emulators.

In 1802, Haynes agreed to stay on as managing partner for seven years, ensuring continuity of management when William Dillwyn acquired the Pottery's leases. With his younger partner Lewis Weston Dillwyn diverted by scientific and other interests, and only periodically engaged directly with Pottery business, Haynes doubtless played a significant role in advising and directing Dillwyn.

Haynes was a considerable figure in Swansea's social and business circles. In 1804 he established Wales's first newspaper, *The Cambrian*. He owned the Cambrian Porter Brewery and had banking partnerships in Swansea, Llanelli and Neath. He was active in municipal affairs, supporting the Swansea Canal and Swansea Harbour, the Glamorgan Library and educational provision, and improvements to paving, lighting and postal services.

William Dillwyn noted that Haynes 'may be rather petulant and vindictive', and indeed Haynes's relationship with Lewis Weston Dillwyn broke down and Haynes left the Pottery in March 1810. Provocatively, right next door to the Pottery, he established the South Wales Soap Works, whose 'unwholesome effluvia' caused Dillwyn to take legal action in 1810 to have it closed down; then, in 1813, Haynes established the rival Glamorgan Pottery. Haynes was declared bankrupt in 1826, when the Haynes & Co banking business failed.

---

[41] Jonathan Gray, 'An American and an American Trader in Wales: Fresh Insights into the Cambrian Pottery, 1789-1810', American Ceramic Circle Journal, volume XVI (2007)

Left: Lewis Weston Dillwyn (see p.136).

Right: Haynes, Dillwyn & Co. trade card, inscribed *1806* © Trustees of the British Museum.

Lewis Weston Dillwyn (1778-1855)

Lewis Weston Dillwyn[42] first came to Swansea in 1802, when his father William Dillwyn (1743-1823) acquired a controlling interest in the Cambrian Pottery. William Dillwyn was born in Chester County, Pennsylvania, but settled in London in 1777, where he was a draper, trading in linens. In 1802 he agreed with George Haynes, a fellow Quaker, to buy much of Haynes's stake in the Cambrian Pottery. Haynes undertook to assist the young Lewis Weston Dillwyn in the management of the business, although it was William's money that funded expansion and investment in new plant.

Lewis Weston Dillwyn was interested in the natural sciences, especially botany, and was frequently in London. He may have been behind the factory's short-lived London retail outlet, the Cambrian Warehouse. In 1807 he married Mary Adams, the daughter (and later heir) of John Llewelyn of Penllergaer, a neighbouring landowner.

In 1808 the couple took a house in Swansea High Street, before moving to the Willows on Mount Pleasant, which was their home until 1818.

In 1810 Dillwyn and Haynes quarrelled, and Dillwyn decided that his managers Timothy and John Bevington should 'undertake jointly the whole management and conduct of the concern, subject only to his own occasional personal superintendence.' Nevertheless, Dillwyn was personally responsible for the manufacture of porcelain in Swansea from 1814. He recruited William Billingsley and Walker and worked on the development of new porcelain bodies. In 1817, his father-in-law John Llewelyn died, leaving Dillwyn to manage the Penllergaer estates. He reluctantly leased both the Cambrian Pottery and the China Works to a new partnership, led by the Bevingtons.

In 1824, Dillwyn resumed management of the Pottery. He supplied new capital investment, but expected his new managers to run the Pottery for him. In 1831 he put his youngest son, Lewis Llewelyn, aged just seventeen, in nominal charge of the Pottery, and in 1836 transferred the business to him. In 1832 he had been elected to the first reformed Parliament as one of the two MPs for Glamorgan, where he was a supporter of Lord Grey's Whig government.

---

[42] Oliver Fairclough, 'Lewis Weston Dillwyn and the Cambrian Pottery' in Jonathan Gray (ed.), *Welsh Ceramics in Context Part 1* (Swansea: Royal Institution of South Wales, 2003), pp. 215-228

Right: The Willows (the house on the left with a prominent bay window), engraved after a drawing of 1818 by Thomas Baxter.

Far right: *Penllergaer House*, by F. H. Dillwyn, bodycolour on paper on card, about 1834.

Thomas Pardoe (1770-1823)

Born in Derby, Thomas Pardoe[43] was apprenticed at the Derby porcelain factory at around 15 years old. When he was 20 years old, he was one of the skilled artisans George Haynes brought to the Cambrian Pottery as he sought to improve the Pottery's output. He became not only the Pottery's chief painter but also, between 1802 and 1804, its acting manager. In 1797 he married the daughter of a local banker and colliery owner; however, he was widowed, and married again in 1802.

Pardoe's work at the Cambrian Pottery shows him to be a remarkably versatile artist, his style having an immediacy and liveliness that was unusual at the time. Best known for his botanical decoration, he painted landscapes and figures, birds and animals, flowers and fruit, shells and east Asian styles with equal aplomb.

In 1809 Pardoe left the Cambrian Pottery to establish his own business in Bristol. His first address there was 'under the Bank', a commercially advantageous location at the centre of Bristol's docks complex. By 1812 he had moved his residence and shop to 28 Bath Street, one of Bristol's grander streets. In Bristol Pardoe decorated pottery and porcelain bought in from Coalport and Staffordshire, often inscribing objects with the date, his name and the customer's name. He won commissions not only in Bristol and Bath but also from Welsh people, such as Sir Richard Philipps of Picton Castle, 1st Baron Milford. He branched out into painting window glass for churches and private houses, and instructing women of leisure in the art of painting china and velvet, and painting in oils.

In 1821 Pardoe returned to Wales to work for his friend William Weston Young at Nantgarw, decorating the remaining stock of porcelain. He painted quickly, so that decorated wares could be sold at a modest premium at auctions arranged by Young in 1821 and 1822. He was nevertheless able to demonstrate his considerable range, and on occasion worked on special commissions, such as lavish services for Young's nephew and for the industrialist Wyndham Lewis.

---

[43] Andrew Renton, 'Thomas Pardoe and William Weston Young' in Jonathan Gray (ed.), *Welsh Ceramics in Context Part I*, (Swansea: Royal Institution of South Wales, 2003), pp. 120-146; Andrew Renton, 'Thomas Pardoe in Bristol' in *English Ceramic Circle Transactions*, 26 (2015), pp. 93-110

Right: Self-portrait by Thomas Pardoe, oil on panel, about 1810-1820.

Far right: Nantgarw ice-cream pail and cover, decorated by Thomas Pardoe, 1818-1823
© Bonhams.

The Leading Figures

William Weston Young (1776-1847)

Born into a Bristol Quaker family, William Weston Young[44] lived a multi-faceted life in which ceramics was only one of many pursuits. In 1797 he set up as a miller and corn merchant near Neath, but went bankrupt in 1802. A year later Lewis Weston Dillwyn employed him as scientific draughtsman for his publication *British Confervae*, and as part-time painter of earthenware at the Cambrian Pottery.

Young's decoration of Swansea pottery is meticulous, and seems to reflect both his own and Dillwyn's intellectual interests. Key subjects were scientifically accurate birds, butterflies and animals, figures and landscapes, and bards and druids reflecting the revival of interest in Wales's cultural heritage. Perhaps most of this was commissioned by Dillwyn or others. He often collaborated with Thomas Pardoe, who carried out the gilding and, occasionally, part of the enamelling.

In 1806, Young left the Cambrian Pottery and, with Dillwyn's support, became an Associate of the Linnaean Society. He started a wreck-raising business, supplemented by farming and milling, quarrying and brick-making, and operating as a general merchant. From 1811, land surveying was his main occupation, by means of which he developed a wide and useful network among the gentry and industrialists of south-east Wales. He retained an amateur enthusiasm for enamelling ceramics, installing his own muffle kiln at home in Newton Nottage in 1809.

Arguably, Young did more than anyone to support the Nantgarw porcelain venture. In 1814 he wrote an unsuccessful bid for government funding on behalf of Billingsley and Walker, lent them at least £600 and helped negotiate their temporary move to Swansea. When Billingsley and Walker returned to Nantgarw in 1817, Young secured substantial funding of £2,100 from his social and business contacts, enabling manufacture to continue until Billingsley and Walker left suddenly in 1820. Left to pick up the pieces, Young engaged Pardoe to decorate the remaining stock for local sale, finally pulling out in 1822 when he was again declared bankrupt.

Young retained a passion for Nantgarw porcelain, and tried in vain in the 1830s and 1840s to recreate the Nantgarw porcelain body with a view to supplying it to manufacturers.

---

[44] Andrew Renton, 'Thomas Pardoe and William Weston Young' in Jonathan Gray (ed.) *Welsh Ceramics in Context Part I* (Swansea: Royal Institution of South Wales, 2003), pp. 120-146

Right: Cambrian Pottery pearlware mug painted by William Weston Young with fallow deer, the buck taken from Thomas Bewick's *A General History of Quadrupeds*, about 1805.

Far right: Swansea porcelain plate, painted and fired at Newton Nottage by William Weston Young with chickweed wintergreen after James Sowerby's *English Botany*, about 1816.

William Billingsley (1758-1828)

William Billingsley[45] was born in Derby where his father, a china painter, was probably working at William Duesbury's porcelain factory. At 16 years old he was apprenticed to Duesbury, and rapidly became Derby's leading flower painter, specializing in the painting of roses. His ambition was to make his own porcelain, and in 1795 he left for Pinxton, a mining village eighteen miles north of Derby where he established a small factory in partnership with the owner of the site, John Coke.

Like all Billingsley's subsequent ventures, the Pinxton factory lacked the capital to produce high-quality soft-paste porcelain in a market dominated by mass-produced earthenwares. In 1799 the Pinxton partnership was dissolved, and Billingsley set up a small china-decorating business in nearby Mansfield, where he worked on porcelain blanks from Pinxton and in 1801-1802 from Paris. He made a second attempt to manufacture porcelain between 1803 and 1807 at Brampton, near Lincoln, but the venture lacked capital, and he and his partners again lost their money.

Now heavily in debt, Billingsley took the name Beeley, and went to Worcester where he was mainly employed on developing experimental porcelain bodies. These included a highly translucent frit porcelain that his employers, Barr, Flight and Barr, judged to be uneconomic to manufacture. Together with his son-in-law Samuel Walker, he left to produce this porcelain for himself at Nantgarw late in 1813. As before, he ran out of money after a few months, and was recruited by Dillwyn to work at Swansea.

Dillwyn developed alternative porcelain bodies, and Billingsley seems to have worked primarily as a decorator and supervisor while in Swansea. In the spring of 1817 he returned to Nantgarw, and with further support from William Weston Young resumed production there. His wares sold well 'in the white' on the London market during 1818 and 1819, but by the spring of 1820 his funds were again exhausted, and he abandoned Nantgarw. His last employer was John Rose, at Coalport, where he died.

---

[45] *Not just a bed of roses: the life & work of the artist, ceramicist and manufacturer William Billingsley (1758-1828)* (Lincoln: Usher Gallery), 1996

Right: Bowl, probably made at the de la Courtille factory in Paris and decorated by Billingsley at Mansfield. His aim during all his attempts to make porcelain was to supplant French imports of this sort.

Far right: Ice pail, Derby porcelain, about 1790, painted by William Billingsley with flowers and fruit in imitation of Sèvres porcelain.

The Leading Figures

Thomas Baxter (1782-1821)

Thomas Baxter[46] was one of the finest china painters of the early nineteenth century; he also worked as an art teacher, engraver and painter of portrait miniatures. He was born in Worcester where his father, also Thomas Baxter, was an enameller and gilder. In 1797 the family moved to London, where Thomas senior established a successful china-decorating business in Gough Square, off Fleet Street. The younger Thomas attended the Royal Academy Schools, and decorated porcelain, mostly from Coalport, for his father. In 1814 he moved with his own young family to Worcester, where he worked for the Flight, Barr and Barr porcelain factory.

In the spring of 1816 Baxter moved to Swansea and was employed as a freelance by the China Works to decorate some of their best cabinet wares, primarily for the London market.

These include pieces painted with birds, shells and flowers, and notably with cupids and neo-classical figures executed in a soft, stippled monochrome. He also undertook most of his own gilding, using a simple but elegant wave scroll motif.

He decorated a dessert service made for Lewis Weston Dillwyn's own use, described on completion in September 1817 as 'the china dessert service painted with garden scenery by Mr. Baxter' (see p. 58). While in Swansea he also painted miniature portraits, including one of Dillwyn, and in June 1818 he published a set of six etchings of views around the town. Soon after, he returned to Worcester, where he worked as an enameller for the Flight, Barr and Barr and Chamberlain factories, and as an art master, until his death.

---

[46] John O. Wilstead and Bernard Morris, *Thomas Baxter: The Swansea Years 1816-1819*, Gomer Press (1997)

Right: A Swansea spill vase (1816-1819) and a Chamberlain's Worcester cup (1819-1821), both painted by Baxter with a cupid in a glass.

Far right: A porcelain plaque painted by Thomas Baxter with a memorial portrait of his friend Charles Francis Bone (1787-1802), after a miniature by the sitter's brother Henry Pierce Bone (1779-1855).

William Pollard (1803-1854)

William Pollard[47] was born in Landore near Swansea and apprenticed at the Swansea China Works, probably at around 13 or 14 years old. Here he was instructed in the art of painting porcelain, most likely by David Evans rather than William Billingsley, who was on the point of returning to Nantgarw. Pollard's style closely resembles that of David Evans, with an emphasis on wild and garden flowers such as speedwells, forget-me-nots, strawberries, heather and the wild or 'Burrows' rose for which he is best known. Along with Evans and Henry Morris, Pollard was responsible for creating what is generally recognised as the distinctively beautiful Swansea style of flower painting.

Pollard was also instrumental in spreading the influence of the Swansea style of decoration. In 1822 he left Swansea and went to work in Stoke-on-Trent at the newly established factory of Henry Daniel. In his familiar manner, he painted a number of factory set patterns as well as impressive non-standard floral decoration.

Leaving the Daniel factory in 1827, Pollard returned to Wales and set up his own decorating and retail business in Carmarthen. Describing himself as 'China Manufacturer, and Dealer in Glass and Earthenware', he sold table wares and tea and coffee services, as well as vases and ornamentalwares.

Much of this was decorated in his own workshop, some apparently by Pollard himself, some by assistants. He occasionally decorated earthenware from the Glamorgan Pottery in Swansea, but mostly used English and French porcelain. Some objects bear his 'Pollard Carmarthen' retailer's mark, including a French vase probably bought by Pollard ready decorated with a subject based on a Byron poem.

In 1832 Pollard transferred to Swansea, where he took out a licence as an auctioneer and took on as his assistant George Beddow, a fellow former painter of Swansea porcelain. In 1846 he closed his business and moved to Burnham on Sea in Somerset, where he died.

---

[47] Andrew Renton, 'The Swansea Diaspora: The later careers of David Evans, Henry Morris and William Pollard' in Jonathan Gray (ed.), *Welsh Ceramics in Context: Part II* (Swansea: Royal Institution of South Wales, 2005), pp. 209-234

Right: A Daniel porcelain teapot and stand painted by William Pollard, about 1824-1827.

Far right: A Swansea cabaret tea service painted by William Pollard, about 1816-1822.

The Leading Figures

William Chambers Junior (1809-1882)

William Chambers[48] junior was born at Valenciennes in France. He was educated at Eton and St John's College, Cambridge. His father had inherited the Stepney Estate, and for a while the family lived in the mansion, Llanelly House. However, Chambers junior could not inherit, as his parents were unmarried at the time of his birth, and he purchased the Hafod estate near Aberystwyth following his father's death in 1855. He lived there from 1857 until 1871, when he was declared bankrupt and forced to sell the estate.

He married Joanna Trant Payne in 1835, with whom he had fourteen children, at least two of whom died in infancy. Chambers junior was an important social and political figure in Llanelli. He was a magistrate, founder of the Llanelly Reform Society and the first Chairman of the Llanelly Board of Health. His founding of the South Wales Pottery, and the building of workers' housing soon after, were significant events for the town and its inhabitants. As a magistrate, he played his part in suppressing the Rebecca Riots, the protests by agricultural workers in response to raised road tolls – although he was suspected of being sympathetic to the cause.

He died at Vernon House, in Britton Ferry. His obituary in the Llanelly Guardian described his love for the town, remarking that 'it is to him that we are indebted for the planting of trees in the various streets of the town ... his idea being to make manufacturing Llanelly as attractive as possible.'

---

[48] Dilys Jenkins, *Llanelly Pottery*, DEB Books, (1968)

Right: Photograph of the South Wales Pottery, 1920s. Carmarthen Museum, Abergwili.

Far right: An engraving of William Chambers junior. © Llyfrgell Genedlaethol Cymru / National Library of Wales.

10 | Manufacturers' Marks

The Welsh pottery and porcelain manufacturers featured here used over seventy factory marks. Nevertheless, many of their wares were sold unmarked, or bear only pattern names or numbers, or workmen's marks. It is often uncertain when a particular factory mark was adopted or discontinued. Factories often accumulated considerable reserves of stock, which was sometimes decorated years after its manufacture, so impressed marks indicate when a piece was formed and fired, while painted and print marks tell us only when a piece was decorated. Bogus Swansea and Nantgarw marks are sometimes found on other porcelains.

These are the more common factory marks.

Cambrian Pottery, Swansea 1768-1870

The earliest wares made (from 1768) at the Swansea Pottery do not have a factory mark, though the word 'Swansea' appears on a few inscribed pieces, confirming their place of manufacture. Late eighteenth-century wares are sometimes impressed with a range of small workmen's marks, among them playing card symbols, a star, a cross, a crescent moon, an ermine tail, single letters and numerals. These were widely used in the industry and are not unique to Swansea.

1. SWANSEA impressed
Although it is often said that this mark was introduced around 1790, it seems more likely that it was adopted around 1804, after Lewis Weston Dillwyn became the principal partner, replacing an occasionally found impressed mark 'GH & Co' for the earlier partnership of George Haynes & Co. It was probably used on pottery until 1810 or 1811 and then on porcelain, alongside other marks, until the mid-1820s.

2. Swansea in script
Some pieces bearing the script mark 'Swansea' in Thomas Pardoe's hand can be dated to the late 1790s, and this mark may have remained in use until about 1808.

3. SWANSEA in script
Usually found in gilt, again in Pardoe's hand, this mark may have been used between about 1802 and 1808.

4. CAMBRIAN in script
Again usually in gilt, this mark may be associated with pieces intended for the short-lived Cambrian Company warehouse in London. If so, it can be dated to 1807-1808.

5. DILLWYN & Co impressed
This mark seems to have been introduced following the withdrawal of George Haynes and the formation of the new partnership with the Bevingtons at the end of 1811, and to have remained in use until Lewis Weston Dillwyn leased the business in 1817. It may have been used at the same time as the impressed mark 'SWANSEA', as the latter was also used on porcelain in 1816-1817.

6. DILLWYN & Co SWANSEA impressed in a horseshoe
Perhaps used as an alternative to number 5 above around 1815-1817, and probably the standard mark from 1824 until about 1830.

7. BEVINGTON & CO. impressed
Dateable to 1817-1824, this mark, and an alternative 'SWANSEA POTTERY BEVINGTON & Co' impressed in a horseshoe, are both very rare, suggesting that the Bevington partnership concentrated mainly on the decoration of earlier stock.

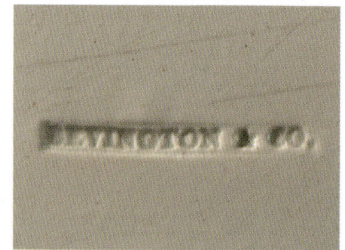

8. DILLWYN SWANSEA impressed in a semi-circle

Seems to have replaced mark number 6. Perhaps introduced about 1825-1830, and then used until 1850. An alternative semi-circular mark of about 1836-1848 is DILLWYN & Co impressed.

Printed marks often combine the pattern name with 'Dillwyn & Co' or 'D & Co'. These include:

9. DILLWYN'S ETRUSCAN WARE printed in a cartouche

Used on the red-bodied 'Etruscan' wares about 1848-50.

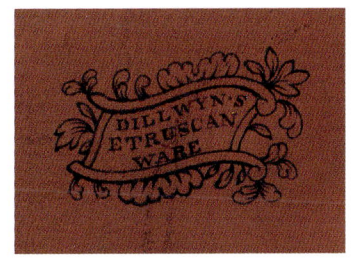

10. EVANS & GLASSON SWANSEA impressed in a triangle

Used together with printed marks by the Evans & Glasson partnership from 1850 to 1862.

11. D.J. EVANS & CO printed above the Prince of Wales's feathers

The final factory mark of 1862-1870 is usually combined with the pattern name.

The Swansea China Works 1814-1826
The first porcelains made at Swansea were probably unmarked, and it was not until May 1817 that Lewis Weston Dillwyn announced that in future the word 'SWANSEA' would be stamped – which could mean either impressed or printed – on every piece. Even after that date some pieces seem to have been sold unmarked or with only a pattern number. These are sometimes prefixed N or No (for number) and mostly fall into the range 100 to 600. Some pieces of Swansea (and Nantgarw) also bear retailer/decorator marks.

12. Swansea in script
Usually, but not always, inscribed in red enamel. Several different hands are known, and these may in some cases be the work of the painter who decorated the piece. Perhaps the earliest type of mark to be used, and uncommon after 1817.

13. SWANSEA transfer-printed or stencilled in red
Probably the most common mark, adopted by the summer of 1816, and probably still in use until the final stock sale nearly ten years later.

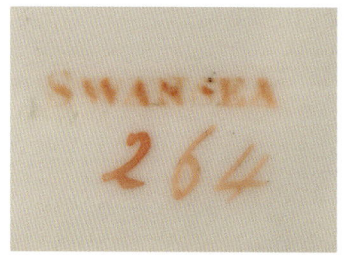

14. SWANSEA impressed
Perhaps associated with the May 1817 announcement about 'stamped' marks. Found on both 'duck-egg' (bone) and 'trident' (soapstone) bodies, sometimes with crossed tridents (or a single trident). Appears to be more common on wares intended for outside decoration.

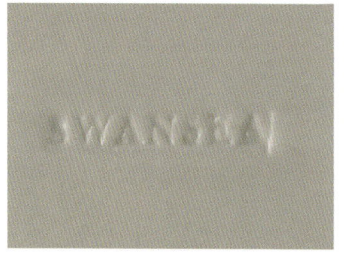

15. DILLWYN & Co impressed
Both this, dating from 1816-17, and a corresponding BEVINGTON & CO mark of 1817-24 (number 16), are very rare. Red stencilled versions of both are also recorded.

16. BEVINGTON & CO. impressed

Nantgarw China Works 1814 and 1816-1823
It is not known whether Billingsley and Walker marked any of the porcelain they made at Nantgarw in 1814. When they resumed production there, impressed marks were often used where practical, as on plates and dishes.

17. NANTGARW and C.W. impressed
Several stamps were used as the name is often hyphenated (NANT-GARW) or the C.W. (for china works) omitted. Sometimes with an incised letter below the mark.

18. Nantgarw in script
A few pieces have a mark in Pardoe's hand, which is probably genuine, but inscribed or printed Nantgarw marks should otherwise be treated with caution.

The Glamorgan Pottery 1813-1838
Most (but not all) pieces have a printed or an impressed mark. Some small workmen's marks were also used.

19. BAKER BEVANS & IRWIN impressed in a horseshoe
Probably used throughout. Also found enclosing the Prince of Wales's feathers or a numeral and with SWANSEA below.

20. BB&I printed in a cartouche
Often with 'Opaque China' or with a pattern name. Found mainly in black or blue.

Manufacturers' Marks

The South Wales Pottery
The firm used a wide range of marks, many incorporating its name.

21. South Wales Pottery impressed in a horseshoe
Used during the Chambers period (1840-1855). Sometimes with the addition of William Chambers, Junior, and/or Llanelly. The initials S.W.P. also used.

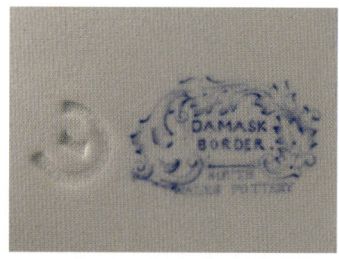

22. Pattern name printed in a cartouche with South Wales Pottery or S.W.P.
The initials C & H were used during the Coombs and Holland period (1855-1858), W.T.H for that of Holland only (1858-1875), and G & D for Guest and Dewsberry (after 1878).

23. 'Llanelly', 'Llanelly Pottery' or 'Llanelly Art Pottery', stencilled
Found on early twentieth-century hand-painted wares.

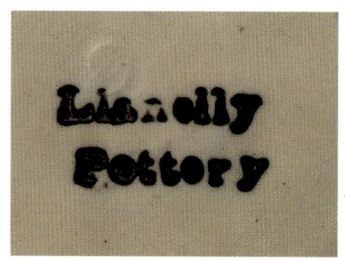

11 | Further Reading

Rachel Conroy, 'The Cambrian Pottery: Dillwyn's Pricelist of 1843', *Transactions of the English Ceramic Circle,* 29 (2018), pp. 117-128

Howell G. M. Edwards, *Swansea and Nantgarw Porcelains: A Scientific Reappraisal*, Springer, 2017

Howell G. M. Edwards, *Nantgarw and Swansea Porcelains: An Analytical Perspective,* Springer, 2018

W. J. Grant-Davidson, *The Pottery of South Wales: An Illustrated Guide*, Mackie, 2010

Jonathan Gray (ed.), *Welsh Ceramics in Context: Part I*, Royal Institute South Wales, 2003

Jonathan Gray (ed.), *Welsh Ceramics in Context: Part II*, Royal Institute South Wales, 2005

Jonathan Gray, 'War & Peace: Swansea Ceramics 1775-1815', *Art Antiques* London 2010, Haughton International, 2010, pp. 31-40: https://www.haughton.com/articles/2010/6/13/war-peace-swansea-ceramics-1775-1815

Jonathan Gray, *The Cambrian Company: Swansea Pottery's London Warehouse 1806-1808*, the author, 2012

Helen L. Hallesy, *The Glamorgan Pottery, Swansea 1814-1838*, Gomer Press, 1995

Gareth Hughes and Robert Pugh, *Llanelly Pottery*, Llanelli Borough Council, 1990

Dilys Jenkins, *Llanelly Pottery*, DEB Books, 1968

W. D. John, *Swansea Porcelain*, The Ceramic Book Company, 1958

W. D. John, *William Billingsley (1758-1828); his outstanding achievements as an artist and porcelain maker*, The Ceramic Book Company, 1968

W. D. John and Catherine Coombes, *Nantgarw Porcelain*, The Ceramic Book Company, 1948

W. D. John, G. J. Coombes and Catherine Coombes, *The Nantgarw Porcelain Album*, The Ceramic Book Company, 1975

A. E. Jones and Leslie Joseph, *Swansea Porcelain: Shapes and Decoration*, D. Brown & Sons, 1988

Ernest Morton Nance, *The Pottery & Porcelain of Swansea & Nantgarw*, Batsford, 1942

John Twichett et al, *Not just a bed of roses: the life & work of the artist, ceramicist and manufacturer William Billingsley (1758-1828)*, Usher Gallery, Lincoln, 1996

Arleen Tanner, Grahame Tanner (ed.), *Swansea's Cambrian Pottery Transferware: and Other Welsh Examples*, Polstead Press, 2005

William Turner, *The ceramics of Swansea and Nantgarw: a history of the factories with biographical notices of the artists and others, notes on the merits of the porcelains, the marks thereon, etc.,* Bemrose & Sons, 1897

Rowland Williams, *Nantgarw Porcelain 1813-1822*, the author, 1993

John O. Wilstead and Bernard Morris, *Thomas Baxter: The Swansea Years 1816-1819*, Gomer Press, 1997